DIVING FOR TREASURE

Whittles Dive Series

editor Rod Macdonald

The Whittles Dive Series is a collection of cutting edge books dealing with every aspect of diving – from exploring lost shipwrecks to cave diving, technical mixed gas and rebreather diving. The Series is edited by internationally acclaimed diving author Rod Macdonald, noted for works such as *Dive Scapa Flow* and *Dive Truk Lagoon*.

Volume 1 *Underwater Potholer: A Cave Diver's Memoirs*
Duncan Price
ISBN 978-184995-158-6

DIVING FOR TREASURE

Discovering history in the depths

VIC VERLINDEN

and

STEFAN PANIS

Whittles Publishing

Published by
Whittles Publishing Ltd.,
Dunbeath,
Caithness, KW6 6EG,
Scotland, UK

www.whittlespublishing.com

© 2018 V. Verlinden & S. Panis
ISBN 978-184995-325-2

CONTENTS

CONTENTS

SS *TUBANTIA*

THE HUNT FOR THE GOLD OF THE *TUBANTIA*

The amount of time and money spent on attempts to salvage the cargo of the Dutch passenger liner *Tubantia* have been far greater than those devoted to any other wreck in the North Sea. The story of the search for the liner's gold is so fascinating that three books and numerous newspaper articles have been published about it, and it has also been the subject of a BBC television documentary. A total of six salvage teams have worked the wreck in attempts to reach its immeasurable treasure.

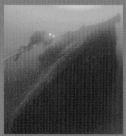

SS *Tubantia*

Owner: Royal Dutch Lloyd/Lloyd Royal Hollandais, Amsterdam

Built: 1914 Alexander Stephen & Sons Ltd, Linthouse near Glasgow

Propulsion: Two quadruple expansion machines, two propellers

Tonnage: 13911 tons

Dimensions: Length 170m, beam 20m

Speed: 16 knots

Passenger accommodation: 252 first class, 236 second class, 135 third class, 854 in huts and in dormitories, 335 crew

The well-appointed first class dining room.

A first class cabin on the *Tubantia*

Previous page top left: A porcelain sink lies among the debris
Previous page bottom left: The impressive bow of the *Tubantia*
Previous page right: A diver films the wreck

DEPARTURE FROM AMSTERDAM

At 13:00 on 15th March 1916, at the height of the First World War, the passenger liner *Tubantia* of the Royal Dutch Lloyd set sail on its eleventh trip from Amsterdam to Buenos Aires. Captain Wijtsma set a course for the lightvessel *Maas*, which it passed at around 21:00. Then he continued on in the direction of Noordhinder Bank. The ship was to anchor there for the night, as daylight was required to navigate nearby minefields. Once anchored, Captain Wijtsma was relieved by first helmsman Vreugdenhill in order to get a few hours' rest in his bunk. At 02:15 a trail of bubbles coming from a torpedo was spotted by fourth helmsman Van Leuven, followed moments later by an enormous explosion amidships on the starboard side. When the captain was notified that the situation was serious he immediately ordered the deployment of the lifeboats for the eighty-seven passengers and 294 crew members.

The ship was severely damaged and started to list. Nevertheless, all passengers and crew were safely transferred to the lifeboats. First helmsman Vreugdenhill performed one final inspection of the ship and noticed that the tables in the first class restaurant had been nicely set for breakfast and had been decorated with fresh flowers. A few hours later everything was at the bottom of the North Sea. The small steamer *Breda* received the distress signal from the *Tubantia* and took on

Captain Wijtsma
The *Tubantia* in the docks at Amsterdam, prior to departure

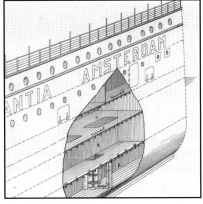

Drawing showing the point of impact of the torpedo

A postcard of the *Tubantia* in all its glory

The steamship *Breda* rescues many passengers

The crew boarding for another voyage.

The ship's bell.

UB13 in Zeebrugge harbour.

Laatste Berichten.

Nederland.

Nederland en de oorlog.

De Tubantia.

Hedenavond 11 uur is een groot aantal van de bemanning en van de passagiers der Tubantia in eenige gereserveerde wagons, welke in den gewonen trein gehaakt waren, uit Hoek van Holland te Amsterdam aangekomen. Het waren de schipbreukelingen, die door het stoomschip Breda uit de sloepen opgepikt waren. Ook de kapitein van de Tubantia, de heer Wijtsma, bevond zich in dezen trein, doch stapte te Haarlem, waar hij woonachtig is, uit. Aan het station werd hij door zijn echtgenoote en eenige familieleden opgewacht. Toen de trein zich in beweging zette, brachten de geredden, die naar Amsterdam doorreisden, hem een warme ovatie.

In den trein spraken wij een lid van het consulaire corps te Madrid, die zich op de Tubantia had ingescheept. Hij vertelde ons, dat hij zich omstreeks half-elf te ruste had begeven; zijn metgezel was tot 3 uur in de rooksalon opgebleven. Kwart over twee werd hij opgeschrikt door een geweldigen slag; hij snelde naar de rooksalon, waar hij dikke rookwolken uit zag opstijgen en een sterke gaslucht waarnam, die trouwens door vele anderen is opgemerkt. Alle pas-

The first newspaper article about the disaster.

The lifeboats on the *Tubantia.*

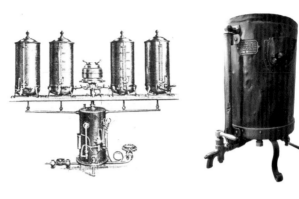

The three kettle system to make tea in the kitchen and alongside a drawing of the arrangement with a clean kettle

board 242 of the shipwrecked persons. The others were taken on board by the ships *Gorredijk* and *La Campine*.

THE INVESTIGATION

After the war an investigation was conducted into the sinking. At the time of the torpedo attack the Netherlands was a neutral country, which made matters worse. Pieces of copper and brass engraved with '2033' were recovered from a damaged lifeboat, proving that the *Tubantia* had been torpedoed. The number 2033 was the serial number of a Schwarzkopf torpedo that had been fired by U-boat *UB-13*, which was under the command of Commander Metz.

TREASURE OF THE *TUBANTIA*

A couple of years after the war, the retired British major Sydney Vincent Sippe was approached by a former spy of the German Empire. Hjalmar Schacht had been in charge of the reforms of the banking sector in Belgium during the war, and had been very close to the top of the German cabinet. He told the story of 13 tons of pure gold that was to be smuggled to South America on orders of the German Emperor. The

The anchor chain.

Micha Govaerts and Agnes Rypens on their way to the *Tubantia*

A chamber pot with logo from the ship

treasure was the personal asset of the Emperor, who realised that Germany might actually lose the war. That is why during a secret operation in Switzerland, the gold was hidden in balls of cheese and loaded on to the *Tubantia*. However, the Germans found out at the last moment that the British Navy had been made aware of its precious cargo and was planning an inspection and so Schacht claimed, it torpedoed the *Tubantia*. Thus, they made sure the treasure would remain out of the hands of the enemy. There were also some very wealthy people among the passengers, including a Mr Vega, Bolivian envoy to Berlin, who lost £150,000 in the disaster.

Sippe, a former war hero and pilot, was interested in the story and together with the Société Maritime Nationale (a shipping agent in Paris) put together an expedition to the wreck to recover the treasure. While Sippe was working over the wreck in 1923, a competitor by the name of Zandudi Landi (one of the most famous salvors of the time) arrived. Landi was backed financially by London businessman C.P. Read. This development caused a small war between the rival boats above the wreck of the

Aft promenade deck

The newspapers follow
the discovery

Tubantia, which was decided in favour of the Landi expedition. Landi used explosives to blast holds 3 and 4, where the gold was thought to be. He tried this several times but yielded no spectacular results. During the following years, several other parties tried to recover the gold, including the Sunderland Salvage Company of Lindsay Swan, Hunter, which used its ship *Reclaimer* in its attempt. On one occasion, after sailing from Ostend to the site after a spell of bad weather, the *Reclaimer* arrived to find the Italian ship *Artiglio*, owned by the Sorima company from Genoa over the wreck. Sorima had earned a big reputation within the salvage world by recovering an enormous load of gold from the wreck of the *Egypt*. However, the *Artiglio* was taken off the operation after just a month due to a lack of success.

Interest in the wreck then waned, although in 1934 the ship's bell was accidently pulled up by a fisherman in one of his nets. Although some expeditions claim to

Gin bottles, a glass citrus press and
porcelain crockery with ship's logo

Bronze portholes

A coffee cup.

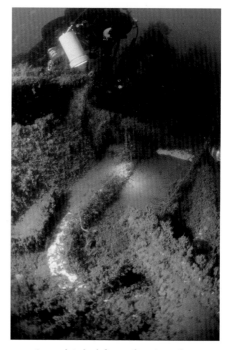

A bronze Buddha after cleaning.

A porcelain bath from a first class cabin.

have recovered valuable cargo, this was never proven. In 1955 the *Tubantia* was mentioned in a book by Sir Robert H. Davis, the director of London-based diving company Siebe Gorman & Co. Ltd, titled *Deep Diving and Submarine Operations*. However, the wreck and the gold were soon forgotten.

DIVING THE *TUBANTIA*

In 1991 the wreck of the *Tubantia* was again front page news when it was rediscovered by Belgian sports divers. The *Tubantia* is situated 35 miles from the Belgian shore at

GPS position 51.49.84N/002.49.08E. The depth ranges from 30 to 38m. The visibility is usually good (2m) to very good (15m), but you need to be on the lookout for discarded fishing nets. Many salvage expeditions involved the use of explosives on the wreck, so it is heavily damaged. The bow with the anchor winch is still the most recognisable part, but the gigantic boilers are also easily identifiable. For the first couple of years after its rediscovery we could still see bronze portholes of all shapes and sizes scattered throughout the wreck during our dives. A bronze sculpture of a Buddha has been recovered, probably from the ladies' salon, but not much has been found of the vast quantities of silverware on board (it probably lies underneath the hull). We could not find any trace of the gold or other valuables either. Still, in his book *The Atlas of Shipwrecks and Treasure* (1995) the famous English wreck hunter Nigel Pickford mentions the wreck of the *Tubantia* as carrying a load of gold and diamonds. The myth of the *Tubantia* will probably bring many divers beautiful dreams about fabulous treasure waiting to be discovered at the bottom of the North Sea.

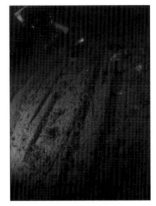

The planks of the promenade deck

A diver in front of the steam boiler

The winch of the *Tubantia*

SS ELBE

PORCELAIN FROM THE DEEP

As first helmsman Robert Henry Craig of the coal steamer SS *Crathie* went for a cup of coffee in the galley, the *Crathie* rammed the luxury German ocean liner SS *Elbe* at full steam.

Above: Captain Van Gossel
*Previous pag*e: The hull,
overgrown by anemones.

SS *Elbe*

Type: Passenger ship

Shipping company: Norddeutscher Lloyd

Built: 1881 John Elder & Co. Glasgow, Scotland

Propulsion: Compound steam engine

Tonnage: 4,510 tons

Dimensions: 136m long, 19m beam

Speed: 17.5 knots

Postdampfer „Elbe"

Nächster Abgang von **Bremen** am
Mittwoch, den 31. August.
Ankunft in **Newyork** voraussichtlich am
am 9-10. September.
Briefe und andere für diesen Dampfer bestimmte
Postsendungen nach Newyork und den Vereinig-
ten Staaten von Nordamerika sind zu adressiren:
über Bremen per „Elbe"
und müssen spätestens **am 30. August**
Abends in **Bremen** eintreffen.
Die Direction
des Norddeutschen Lloyd.

Advertisement for a crossing.

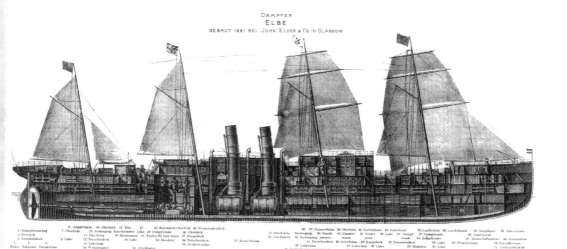

Beautifully detailed view of the cross-section of the *Elbe* on which the
steam engines and different sections are clearly visible.

It was a bitter −19°C when Captain Van Gossel did his last inspection of his ship before setting sail to New York from the port of Bremerhaven, Germany, on the night of 30th January 1895. The SS *Elbe* was a fast ocean-going liner of 4,510 tons and was carrying, among other things, a cargo of rice, iron parts and a precious load of Rudolstadt porcelain for the American market. Also on board were a large number of postal bags containing valuable bonds, money and diamonds. Among the fifty first class passengers out of a total of 354 were the Guttman brothers. These former directors of a flour factory were carrying 300,000 Dutch guilders on their voyage to New York. The ship was to make a short stop at Southampton, England, to take on additional passengers, before continuing on her route to New York.

She cast off from Bremerhaven at around 15:00, and started her voyage across the North Sea under the guidance of both a German and an English pilot.

THE COLLISION

The SS *Elbe*, with her 5,600hp steam engine, was capable of a top speed of 17.5 knots. When night fell, Captain Van Gossel gave the order to fire off signalling flares at regular intervals to warn other vessels of her proximity. She was also lit up by hundreds of electrical lights on the side of the ship, making her clearly visible under normal circumstances.

A sister ship at the Antwerp docks.

Promenade deck.

During the night the south-easterly wind picked up, sometimes reaching gusts of Beaufort force 6, and any seawater washing her deck froze immediately. At around 05:20 officers on the bridge noticed another ship approaching. It was the coal ship SS *Crathie* on her way from Rotterdam to Aberdeen, Scotland. The ship was under the command of Captain Gordon, who at that moment had just retired to his bunk for a few hours' sleep, leaving the ship in the hands of first helmsman Robert Henry Craig. Craig left his station to get a cup of coffee from the galley, leaving only the helmsman on the bridge. The helmsman did not notice the fast approaching *Elbe*, and a few moments later the *Crathie* rammed the stately passenger liner full force on the starboard side, just aft of the steam boilers.

EVERYONE FIGHTS FOR THEIR LIFE

On the smaller *Crathie*, the steam engine was put into reverse to break loose from the liner. The coal ship was severely damaged around the bow but was still afloat, so the captain gave the order to return to Rotterdam – unaware of the dramatic developments unfolding aboard the *Elbe*. Captain Van Gossel immediately gave the order to close the watertight doors on the partitioning bulkheads. These bulkheads, however, did not reach the main deck (the normal requirement for

The *Crathie*, which rammed the *Elbe*.

Glass jug.

passenger liners). Attempts were immediately made to deploy the lifeboats, but they were frozen to the davits and needed to be hacked free. The crew succeeded in releasing two lifeboats, although the first one was immediately smashed to pieces against the hull of the ship. A German lady-in-waiting, Anna Boecker, was in this lifeboat and ended up in the freezing water, but was pulled into the second lifeboat by a helping hand. This made her the only woman to survive the drama. The English fishing boat *Wildflower* from Lowestoft took on board twenty survivors six hours later. Among them were five passengers, thirteen crew members and the two pilots. Captain Van Gossel stayed on the bridge until the very last moment

Side view of the hull.

Above left: The logo.
Above right: The signalling gun.

The dive team: Stefan, Nico, Micha and Vic.

and was one of the 332 people on board who did not survive the disaster. Twenty short minutes after the collision, the majestic *Elbe* sunk. On the *Crathie*, only one of the twelve crew and passengers was injured.

INVESTIGATION INTO THE DISASTER

On arrival in the port of Rotterdam, the *Crathie* was immediately detained as the investigation into the cause of the collision got under way.

Captain Gordon and the first helmsman were convicted by a court in Rotterdam and their sailing certifications were revoked indefinitely. The *Crathie* was eventually allowed to return to England. The investigation also brought to light shortcomings on the side of the *Elbe*, such as the deficient watertight partitioning bulkheads and the failure to rehearse boat drills. German and English newspapers continued to report on the sinking for months after the event.

DIVING THE *ELBE*

A wreck that would eventually be identified as the *Elbe* was located by a fisherman from Scheveningen in 1971, who gave its location to members of dive club Sirene, from The Hague. These divers gave her the nickname 'Porthole Wreck' and visited her frequently, recovering hundreds of silver and porcelain items in the following years. Paul De Keijze was finally able to positively identify the wreck after researching in shipping archives and he also placed at my disposal photos of the artefacts. The wreck is located at an average depth of 35m on position 52.35.544north/ 003.27.081east. The bow and the boilers are still clearly recognisable.

Beautifully ornate items are still frequently found on the wreck.

SS *JUSTICIA*

THE DUTCH
TITANIC

Originally named the *Statendam*, this ocean liner was
built for the Holland America Line and was destined to
carry passengers across the Atlantic in great luxury.
However, the First World War was to give a completely
different purpose to this remarkable Dutch ship.

Statendam/SS *Justicia*

Type: Passenger ship
Built: Harland & Wolff Shipyard, Belfast 1914
Shipping company: Holland America Line, built as Statendam II
Propulsion: Steam engine and propellers
Tonnage: 35,000 tons
Dimensions: Length 225m, beam 26m

Building the magnificent ship.
Previous page: Bow of the *Justicia*.

When the Holland America Line ordered a new ship from the Harland & Wolff shipyard in Belfast there was no inkling of the approach of the First World War. The ship was to be the flagship of the shipping company, and it was to be decorated to the highest standards. She was launched, accompanied by huge festivities, on 9th July 1914. She was requisitioned by the British Admiralty at the outbreak of war, and her outfitting was delayed. The *Statendam* was finished as a troop transport ship and rechristened the

Justicia by the Cunard Line. In April 1917 the ship was handed over to the White Star Line and the crew of the *Britannic* (sunk November 1916) was put on board to run her. The *Justicia* was now operational and immediately began transporting troops to and from Australia and New Zealand.

THE ATTACK

The *Justicia* was subsequently chartered by the USA to transport troops to Europe under the command of Captain Hambleton. By 19th July 1918 the ship had already transported 10,000 men and was on her way back to New York when she was attacked by the German U-boat *UB-64* under the command of Otto von Schrader, who was determined to sink her.

After manoeuvring into the right position, he fired the first torpedo, which detonated near the engine room. The *Justicia* remained afloat and arrangements were made for her to be towed to the nearest port. Von Schrader had ordered his submarine to submerge immediately after the attack but instead of breaking off the attack, he waited for a chance to finish her off. The U-boat commander had already sunk sixty-three enemy ships in his career, and had the patience needed to administer the fatal blow. As he approached without being noticed, he fired off two more torpedoes. One missed and the second one was diverted by cannon fire from the *Justicia*. Escort destroyers began hunting the submarine and attacked with depth charges. *UB-64* pressed home its attack, firing off torpedo after torpedo, two of which struck its target. Once *UB-64* had used up all its torpedoes it withdrew from the contact.

The *Justicia* now lies off the beautiful north-west coast of Ireland.

The first dive.

The ship just after the attack.

THE FINAL BLOW

On 20th July the *Justicia* was still under tow to port for repairs and, just as it seemed she was going to survive the attacks, she was attacked again by a different U-boat. This time it was *U-124*, commanded by Commander Hans Oskar Wutsdorff, who despite the many destroyers and accompanying ships, began his attack to administer the final blow and sink the *Justicia*. He carefully steered his submarine through as many as thirty other ships and fired off two torpedoes in quick succession, both striking their target. The *Justicia* was now taking on too much water and it quickly became clear that she was going to sink. The captain immediately ordered the crew to abandon ship and the more than 450 passengers were taken off by other ships. Slowly the liner started sinking, and a short while later the fate of the vessel that was intended to sail the oceans as a floating palace was sealed.

DIVE IN THE OPEN OCEAN

It is wise to always take into consideration the weather when booking a trip to dive the deep wrecks off the north coast of Ireland because most of them are quite a

Above left: The *Loyal Watcher.*
Above right: Preparing to dive.

Retrieving the ship's bell is always an emotional moment.

distance from shore, leaving no shelter from the Atlantic swell.

On the first day of our expedition in 2010 we chose to dive the wreck the furthest offshore, a submarine, with the *Justicia* planned for the next day. However, during the night the wind picked up and by the time we got up in the morning there was a fresh force 5 wind blowing, with a wave height of more than a metre. Still, Darren (captain of our boat, the *Loyal Watcher*) wanted to try to reach the wreck and we would decide on arrival at the wreck site whether or not to dive. The wind did not let up and the wave height also remained the same, so I was faced with the dilemma of whether to dive or not. I decided, with a few others, to give it a try with my expensive camera and all. This would probably be the only chance we would have to dive this wreck during this trip and I definitely wanted to give it a go. I attempted to focus as much as possible while putting on my drysuit and prepping my rebreather, as I didn't want to make any mistakes or forget to do anything. After about half an hour I was done with my preparations, and after one final check of my underwater camera I was ready to jump into the sea. The wave height had now increased to more than 1.5m, and I had to be heavily supported to make my way to the platform so I could jump into the water. When I got the sign from Linda, the captain's wife, my buddy Karl van der Auwera and I jumped overboard and floated towards the shot line to start our descent.

Front view of the bow of the *Justicia*.

Top view of the bow of the *Justicia*.

The winch.

EXPLORING THE BOW

We could already see the wreck beneath us from a depth of 45m, and when we got to the bottom the horizontal visibility was at least 20m.

Portholes in the side of the wreck.

We were somewhere in the middle of the wreck and I could not find my bearings. Luckily, there was another dive team nearby and Wouter Groenewegen, who had dived this wreck many times before, pointed us in the right direction. The bow, still nicely upright, was the most photogenic spot of the wreck. I hadn't brought a tripod with me to photograph it so I had to keep my camera as still as possible while having the shutter open for a few seconds on a long exposure. I took six shots like this, hoping one of them would be good. I then took some shots of the big anchor that was still hanging off the hawsepipe on the bow. We now ascended 8m and continued our exploration of the wreck on the topside of the bow, where we could see the heavy anchor chains lying in the guideways. As we only had a bottom time of twenty-two minutes, we started to swim back towards the shot line, where we passed one of the winches. Everywhere we could see portholes still attached to the collapsed sides of the hull, and there was no end to the debris field for as far as we could see. This was the biggest passenger liner I have ever dived. The debris field was at least 250m long and 50m wide, making it impossible to see it all on one dive. I would happily have spent more time on this beautiful wreck but your tissues get saturated with breathing gas very quickly at a depth of 70m. I looked up along the shot line at least 25m above me and could already see two team members doing their decompression. When I finally stuck my head

Side of the wreck.

Bow.

Starboard anchor.

Hull.

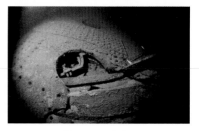

Bronze porthole.

above water after a dive of more than two hours the winds had picked up even more, making climbing up the ladder of the boat not much fun.

This also turned out to be the last dive in Ireland because we were forced to return to Scotland due to the bad weather. I was, however, determined to return to the beautiful wrecks around Malin Head.

RETURN TO THE DUTCH *TITANIC*

In 2011 we once again planned a trip to the wreck of the *Justicia*. My diving buddy on this expedition was Frank Robert, a passionate rebreather diver with more than enough experience diving great depths. It was still early in the morning when we started making our way out to the wreck. Luckily, the seas were a lot calmer than on the previous trip, and we could keep ourselves occupied preparing our equipment. After a couple of hours we were above the wreck and Frank and I jumped in as the first team. The visibility on the wreck wasn't as good as the year before, but it was still pretty reasonable. After we made a tour around the impressive bow, we headed amidships. Here we could see many bronze windows with the glass still in them. The wreck was well broken up in this spot but there were still some walls that were standing up straight with a height of 10m. Around the engine room we also saw numerous heavy bronze pipes and pumps. Time goes fast at a depth of 70m and it was soon time to make our way back to the ascent line and start our decompression. The *Justicia* is one of the most impressive wrecks I've ever dived.

THE GOLD SEEKERS OF THE

RENATE LEONHARDT

The *Renate Leonhardt* was merely an insignificant little steamer when she was torpedoed in 1917 off the Dutch coast near Den Helder. Back then no one could suspect that the ship would become one of the most talked about shipwrecks in Dutch history.

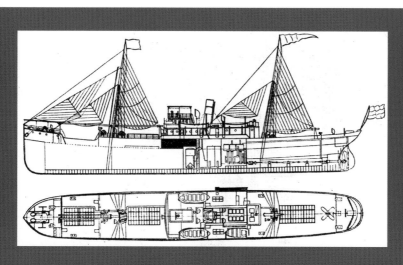

The *Renate Leonhardt*

Type: Freighter

Built: Flensburg Machinery GmBH

Owner: Shipping company Leonhardt & Blumberg Bereederungs GmbH & Co. KG, Germany

Propulsion: Steam engine and propeller

Tonnage: 1,055 tons

Dimensions: Length 60m, beam 8m

Speed: 11 knots

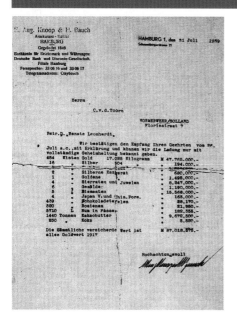

Left: The bill of lading.
Previous page left: diver on the wreck.
Previous page top right: divers near the buoy.
Previous page bottom right: reconnaisance of the wreck.

Rescue attempts for the *Renate Leonhardt*.

The *Renate Leonhardt* is on top of a sandbank.

The *Renate Leonhardt* was built by Flensburg Machinery GmBH in 1889 as a combined steam and sailing ship. The vessel, measuring just 60m long and weighing 1,055 tons, was christened *Brunhilde*. A few years later, and after a significant refitting, she was re-christened *Grenthe Gronau*. Finally, the ship was re-christened *Renate Leonhardt* and entered service as a small freighter on the North Sea.

Sailing for the German shipping company Leonhardt & Blumberg, the *Renate* left Ijmuiden in the Netherlands on 19th August 1917 for Hamburg. The ship was filled to the brim with a cargo of cocoa butter, coal and rum. The following day, the ship was a couple of miles off the coast of Den Helder when she was spotted by a British submarine, which immediately fired off a torpedo. The torpedo hit amidships, blowing a big hole in the hull, and the ship started listing. The explosion killed stoker August Undlaube, but survivors, such as stoker Georged Paul Wolf, were picked up by a Dutch torpedo boat and taken to Niewendiep. There they were offered shelter and a hot meal. A woman who had been taken out of the water unconscious and died on the way to shore was later identified as a Mrs Grosstuck.

After firing its torpedo, the British submarine surfaced to check for survivors, but immediately submerged on seeing the Dutch torpedo boat. After a brief struggle the *Renate Leonhardt* sank to a depth of 22m.

WAS THERE GOLD ON BOARD?

Not long after the torpedoing, rumours started circulating that the *Renate* had been carrying a cargo of gold. Apparently, the crew had seen 454 crates being taken on board while loading the cargo at night. According to the sailors, these were brought over on a barge by German officers, taken to a small spare bunker underneath the bridge, and covered up with a load of coal. Even though there was no hard evidence for this theory, there was at least one person who believed the story. Piet Visser was a fruit farmer from the hamlet of Wijde Wormer, and he was convinced beyond any doubt that there was a treasure of gold in the wreck.

In those days locating a wreck wasn't easy, but when a shipment of cocoa butter washed up on the beach of Egmond aan Zee in 1936, he thought it must have come from the wreck of the *Renate Leonhardt* and was determined to find it. It was,

There was a lot of media attention for Piet Visser's initiative.

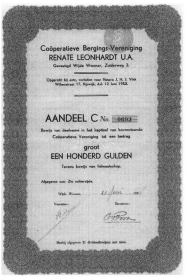

A share for fundraising.

Advertisement with shares for sale

as is quite often the case, fishermen who pointed out to the fruit farmer that there was a wreck filled with coal near the Molengat, approximately 8km from Den Helder. The vessel was located in August 1939 and marked with a buoy.

Working on the wreck was impossible during the Second World War, and salvors then had to wait for the area to be cleared of mines before boats could sail there. On 10th September 1949, P. Van De Schans, a diver contracted by Visser, dived the wreck to do some reconnaissance work. In his report it says he only saw part of the mast and some other parts. He also spoke of a fine clay layer covering the rest of the wreck. He declared in his report: 'I have not seen anything else and I suspect this wreck is lying deep beneath the sand and clay layer.' Nothing was found indicating this wreck was the *Renate Leonhardt* and diving was stopped.

THE TOWER OF THE GOLD FISHERMEN

Visser didn't give up hope on finding gold. He started a co-operative association with his partner, C. Van Der Toorn, to come up with initial capital so the treasure could be extracted from the wreck. In order to raise the necessary funds of 400,000 Dutch guilders shares of 25, 50, 100, 500 and 1,000 guilders were issued. More than 3,000 people from all areas of society expressed interest. Many bought the shares with their last savings in the hope of at least doubling their investments once the gold was recovered. Oil exploration in the Gulf of Mexico gave Visser the idea of building a steel tower and placing it over the wreck. According to the sketches, the tower was to be more than 20m tall and would be towed to the wreck and sunk there.

To sink it the ballast tanks would be opened, allowing the 80-ton tower to rest on the seabed over the wreck. By creating an overpressure in a working chamber at the bottom of the tower, it would be possible to work on the wreck in the dry caisson. That was Visser's plan, and it was what most of the funds raised from the sale of the shares were used for. The tower was ordered in May 1954 from the Hogeveen company and was towed to Ijmuiden on 16th May 1955 for concrete to be poured between the walls of the structure. The total costs at that moment were approximately 250,000 guilders. An open shaft of about 1.7m was also dug, which was to lead to the spare bunker believed to contain the crates of gold. However, before the huge construction could leave port it had to be approved by the Dutch equivalent of the Health and Safety Executive, and it had major concerns about the endeavour. It felt the tower did not meet safety standards and was completely unsuitable for its intended purpose. Among other issues, emergency lighting had to be installed, and the pumps were too light so heavier ones had to be used. The tower also had to be painted on the inside and a ship's phone had to be installed in the working chamber. All this would cost another 50,000 guilders but the society did not have sufficient additional funds.

The tower slowly rusted away in the port of Ijmuiden while Visser looked for a way to raise enough money to complete the project. By now he had lost a lot of his credibility and even the newspapers turned against him, pointing out that the money had been spent on a project of obscene proportions that would never succeed; 500,000 guilders had gone up in smoke and not a sliver of gold had been brought to the surface. Visser was also accused of using outdated techniques, such as dowsing rods instead of modern radio bearings and the Decca Navigator System. Later, the tower that so many had sunk their hard-earned savings into was demolished and sold for scrap metal. Visser had held the whole of the Netherlands in suspense for more than thirty years with the story of the fabulous treasure on the bottom of the North Sea. Never before had so many level-headed Dutchmen believed in an almost impossible story that was supposed to make them rich.

A total of seven lawsuits were brought against Visser for fraud and even attempted manslaughter, but no liability could be proven. The 17,000kg of gold may still be inside the wreck, or it possibly never even existed. This is where the tale of the tower of the gold fishermen ends, but the story of the *Renate Leonhardt* was far from over.

ONLY A FEW METRES AWAY FROM 72 MILLION GUILDERS

In the winter of 1965 two Swiss divers received a tip from the American treasure hunter Harry Rieseberg that a wreck with an enormous treasure of gold was located off the coast of the Netherlands. Rieseberg published the very successful book *600 Milliards Sous les Mers (600 Billion Under the Sea)* in 1948.

In this book he described how he searched all over the world for treasures of gold and artefacts inside shipwrecks. He had some fame in this field, but his stories

C. Van Der Toorn, partner of Piet Visser.

weren't always considered credible by underwater archaeologists and other treasure hunters. Nevertheless, it was reason enough for the brothers Peter and Arnold Sandmeier to take an interest in the story. They were professional divers who mainly concentrated on salvage work in the various lakes and rivers of Switzerland, but sometimes worked abroad. Together with acquaintance Hans-Jurg Schneider, they left for the Netherlands to size up the situation about the true events surrounding the *Renate Leonhardt*.

Once in Den Helder, it soon became clear that Visser still had the salvage rights for the wreck and a decision was made to strike a deal with him. A contract was drafted stating that all finds would be split fifty-fifty and that the contract would be valid for ten years. The Sandmeiers first had a go at it using their own modest means, but quickly discovered that the fickle North Sea is no Swiss mountain lake. They rented a small boat from a local skipper named Boon, from Den Oever, and eventually they succeeded in positioning a buoy over the wreck. It also became apparent that in this specific location in the North Sea the currents could be very strong and that sometimes there wasn't even a slack window.

A period of calm weather came in September and the visibility on the wreck reached 4m; they could finally get their bearings in the cluster of steel and wreckage. At one point they saw a rise in the terrain and they were convinced this must have been the bridge. In the same area they also found a piece of handrail with the name *Brunhilde* on it. They now started to focus on the work around the bridge and they succeeded in breaking open a dividing wall. They thought the treasure couldn't be far away.

Newspaper article.

Cor Janbroers, present day.

Cor Janbroers in his younger
years as an enthusiastic diver.

Using their torches, they could now see a hold that was several metres deep, and when they descended into it they saw a manhole they were able to wrench open using an iron rod. Under this manhole they saw a heavy wooden casing that they weren't able to force open. After about ten minutes it was clear to them that they needed heavier equipment to get the job done, and they ascended to the surface. At that moment they were convinced that they were only a couple of metres away from the 72 million guilders in gold bullion. However, heavier equipment also meant bigger investments, which they couldn't afford. It was decided that other investors were needed so they would be able to continue the search.

An article appeared in a Zurich newspaper and several people came forward who wanted to take a risk for a share of the proceeds of the gold. One of the investors was Mrs Hoechner, a Swiss woman from Hattem in the Netherlands. She became the head sponsor of the entire endeavour. At this point Schneider was forced to leave the enterprise after he was caught issuing false invoices for several purchases.

Around this time the Sandmeiers bought a salvage vessel; however, the engine needed to be repaired and, as it was now winter, working in the North Sea was impossible anyway. The money raised in Switzerland was slow to reach the Netherlands and the brothers had a hard time making ends meet.

IT HAS TO HAPPEN NOW!

The repairs to the engine took longer than expected and in the end it was January 1966 before diving could resume. Divers with any experience in the North Sea would have known that it is only during the summer months that the conditions are good enough to attempt such an endeavour. However, the two brothers had no such experience, and they immediately discovered that visibility was near zero at the time of year. To make matters worse, Arnold developed an inflammation in one of his

Articles that were published about the treasure.

joints and was unable to dive, leaving Peter to finish the task by himself.

By securing a fixed line from their boat to the wreck, he would be able to be lowered down in a cage, which would protect him from the fierce currents. The first dive was an outright disaster, as Peter discovered that the bridge was twisted and an enormous amount of sand had been stacked up in the spot where they believed the gold to be. Only a bit of nylon cord that they had attached to the bridge the year before remained to be seen, but the end disappeared underneath the sand. The following month, another couple of attempts were made but it soon became apparent that it was impossible to reach the gold this way. The weather remained unfavourable and made further attempts impossible. The last attempt was made on the 20th February, but again the bridge, their only reference point, could not be located. No more money was being sent from Switzerland and the cash register was definitely empty. Mrs Hoechner wanted to go into business with a different salvage company and offered the two brothers 500 guilders to pay for their way back to Switzerland. This was a bitter pill to swallow for the men who had claimed at one point to have been only a couple of metres away from the 72 million guilders. The disintegration of the wreck meant, according to them, that all was now lost and that the treasure would forever remained buried underneath the sands of the North Sea. In the end, Arnold said in an interview: 'I'd rather work in a tropical sea where the sharks swim around you than with the human sharks haunting the *Renate Leonhardt*.' Sometime later the boat that had been used was used to pay for the society's outstanding debts.

NEW CANDIDATES SHOW UP

In April 1966 another attempt to dive the wreck was made by two divers from Den Helder, Jan Von Zon and Frans de Groot, allegedly funded by Mrs Hoechner. No further information was revealed about their attempt and we can only assume they were unsuccessful.

When I was researching into the *Renate Leonhardt*, I received an email from Cor Janbroers, who told me he had also dived the wreck in that period. The trip had been organised by a friend who had some money to spare for a couple of trips.

Also on board were two gentlemen from the hydrographical service, who were there to take certain measurements. In total, Cor and his friends dived the wreck eight times without any success – so no other expeditions were carried out after that. As I didn't know Cor personally I asked him if he was still diving. He sent me a message saying he was going to be eighty years old the following month!

THE PRESS TAKES NOTICE

In October 1967 there was some interest from the Dutch magazine *Nieuwe Revu* in organising another search for the wreck and to determine once and for all if the story about the gold was true or not. For this, two professional divers, Jan Vos and Gerrit Driehuis, and one recreational diver, Dr Huib Knook, were asked to investigate it. First-class diver Knook was an editor of the *Sportsdiver* magazine in 1966–67, during which time he wrote the booklet *Underwater for You*. He also had an underwater camera, meaning he would be able to take photos and collect evidence. According to a report by Captain August Methling of the *Renate Leonhardt*, besides the crates of gold on board, there were also paintings, three boxes of diamonds

The trip in 1967.

and eighteen crates of art. One of the two witnesses to the loading of the cargo had died but *Revu* succeeded in tracking down a third crew member who was still alive. Georged Paul Wolf, one of the former stokers of the *Renate*, couldn't help the reporters any further, and the other survivor, Lanser, wouldn't give any more information about the wreck or the treasure.

However, *Revu* persisted with the search. The sea was smooth and it was a sunny day when its divers left the port of Den Helder. The wreck had been marked out using four buoys, one of them a signalling buoy from the pilot service and one was an old sea mine, from which Vos descended to the wreck. His first attempt of photographing the ship failed because the visibility was so

The dive team.

poor. The team decided to wait until the following weekend because then there would be a slack tide and the chances of better visibility would be greater. One week later, Vos and Knook succeeded in taking a couple of shots of the wreck, and they also surfaced with some piping from the condenser. Normally the condenser is located deep in the engine room of the ship, so this now being accessible to divers was a bad omen. It meant the ship had been completely ripped apart, something the divers confirmed. Nothing could be found of the bow section, so it quickly became clear to *Revu* and to the divers that even if the treasure had existed it would never be found.

Knook said of his dive: 'While I descended along the line of the signalling buoy

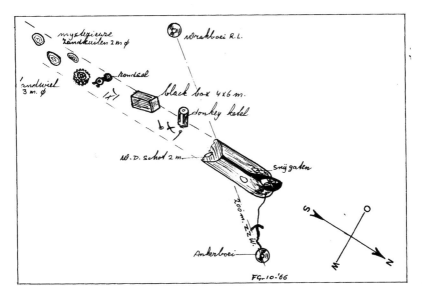

Position of the wreck.

Coen Onstwedder on the helm.

the visibility dropped to under 2m and the deeper I went, the darker it got until I hit the wreck. The wreck is covered all over by sea anemones in all colours. I found myself at 23m deep. Through the forest of sea anemones I could make out the fastening nuts of the crankshaft and a little farther on I could see the piping of the condenser. Other than that it was impossible to make out any shape of the ship.'

Driehuis, who had dived the wreck, confirmed that the midship section was completely ripped apart and that the stern section was lying upside down. The seabed was thoroughly searched within a 150m radius of the wreck but not a single clue was found regarding the treasure or the gold. The diver made these trips on the basis that if nothing was found, he would also receive no payment. Afterwards, he declared that the gold had possibly already been salvaged during the 1930s and that this was why the wreck was so heavily damaged. The *Revu* expedition lasted two days and it had managed to photograph the wreck, which in itself was a huge success for the divers involved and for the magazine, which could now publish a full report.

Almost ten years later, another interview with Visser was published in the *Algemeen Dagblad* of 31st December 1976. By then he had been hunting the treasure for forty years. The reason for the interview was that the Van den Akker company from Rotterdam had carried out an investigation using an echo sounder, which revealed more uninvestigated parts of the wreck.

Visser was still convinced there had been gold, but that others got to it first. He told the newspaper *Algemeen Dagblad*: 'They called me a Gold Prophet, a conman, a criminal and more. I am accused of embezzling all of the money, but when I had to show my accounts to the court, everything was in order.' In 1974 Visser was told by divers that the treasure wasn't there any more, and he asked the public prosecutor in Amsterdam for an enquiry. The answer he received was: 'There is no point doing an investigation and I also think it wouldn't be possible to do one.' I haven't been able to find any reference to Visser after this, so he may have died.

THE WRECK IN 2008

For years John Neuschwander was the editor-in-chief of the Dutch magazine *Duiken*. He was an enthusiastic diver and also collected anything to do with shipwrecks. Sadly, he died suddenly in 2005, which was a shock to me because we had known each other for years. After writing several articles on shipwrecks in the North Sea for *Duiken*, I unexpectedly came into the possession of John's shipwreck archives. Over the course of thirty years he had collected everything on the subject and it therefore held a wealth of information.

One of the files dealt with the wreck of the *Renate Leonhardt*, which drew my attention because of the extraordinary story. During my research I got into contact with Hans Eelman, who lived on the island of Texel. Hans was a famous wreckhunter, who over the years has found many special wrecks around his area. In an email he told me he had also dived the wreck about twenty years earlier (around 1986). During these dives he could clearly identify the double bottom, some salvage equipment that had been left behind on the seabed, a boiler, and a big fishing net. This was the extent of his report. I was determined to dive the wreck myself, so I therefore got in touch with Coen Onstwedder of the North Sea Divers Club in Den Helder. Coen is a real North Sea wreck diver and he was willing to take me to the site. However, when we finally picked a date, the dive had to be called off the night before because there was too much wind.

Finally, on 16th August, my wife Agnes and I drove the 250km to the port of Den Helder, which was where we were to meet up with Coen and his dive team. The weather had thankfully remained stable so the dive could go ahead. Coen's boat was an almost brand new motor cruiser about 6.5m long, which had enough space

Coen Onstwedder's new motor cruiser.

The divers carefully get ready.

The dive begins.

to comfortably accommodate four divers and a powerful 135hp diesel engine.

As the wreck was situated not far from shore, we were anchored on it after about an hour and we got ready for the dive. My buddy for this dive was Peter Vet, who used double 10-litre cylinders. I was going to dive with my Inspiration rebreather and carry an 11-litre bailout cylinder. Following a fifteen-minute wait, it was finally slack water and we could go diving. After all the stories I had read about the wreck I was a bit tense; suppose we were to find a bar of gold on the wreck after all! I tried to keep my mind on the dive because a rebreather is a computer-controlled unit that still needs to be monitored.

FINALLY ON THE WRECK MYSELF!

I jumped into the water immediately after Peter and held on tightly to the rope that would take me to the descent line, as there was still a strong current running. Fortunately, I had made a last-minute decision to first do a survey of the wreck without taking my camera. A rebreather and a bailout cylinder create a lot of drag in a current and this was very noticeable. It took a serious amount of work to make it down the line and I had to take breaks on the way down to avoid getting out of breath.

After about five minutes I finally made it to the wreck and the visibility was about 2m with a lot of plankton in the water. Since I saw that it might have been possible to take photos, I decided to return to the boat and to get my camera. The return only took a minute because the current took me with it but once I made it to the boat I had to hold on tight or I would have been washed away. Carrying the camera made my return journey to the wreck even tougher. Still, I made it, and once there I found a sheltered spot in which to set up my camera.

Before I started taking pictures I checked to see if my rebreather was still okay. Peter had used a reel, so I could follow the line to where he was and there I immediately recognised the crankshaft Vos and Knook had mentioned. The visibility wasn't ideal but it wasn't going to get any better either, and this was my only chance to take some photos. A few metres on I could clearly make out the round shapes of the boiler but here the visibility was too poor for photography. There were also huge pieces of fishing nets on the wreck so it was important not to progress too quickly. Every time we advanced a couple of metres we had to use our lights to check that we weren't inadvertently swimming into fishing nets. This could have disastrous consequences on the bottom of the North Sea and I knew a couple of divers who hadn't survived such an incident.

The wreck was also inhabited by enormous crabs and you don't want to accidentally pick these up by the claws as they have tremendous strength in them. After thirty minutes we had had enough and started making our way back to the ascent line. While Peter was reeling in his line I took a few more photos and looked around again to see if there was a bar of gold to be found. Unfortunately, this wasn't the case, but I still had an enormous feeling of satisfaction as I slowly started my ascent. I had successfully dived the wreck that had held a large portion of the Dutch population in its spell for half a century.

SS *DRUMMOND CASTLE*

ON THE WAY TO HER DOOM

The most famous shipwreck off the coast of Brittany is without a doubt the passenger liner *Drummond Castle*. More than 100 years since the ship crashed into cliffs at the south entrance to the Fronveur Sound, the memory is still kept alive by the people of Molene.

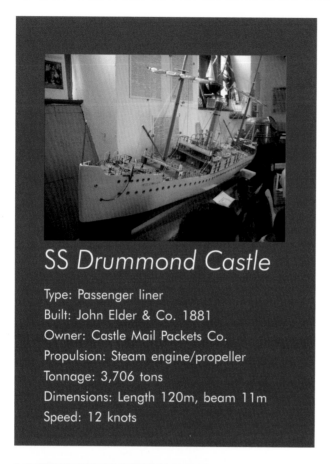

SS Drummond Castle

Type: Passenger liner

Built: John Elder & Co. 1881

Owner: Castle Mail Packets Co.

Propulsion: Steam engine/propeller

Tonnage: 3,706 tons

Dimensions: Length 120m, beam 11m

Speed: 12 knots

WRECK OF THE DRUMMOND CASTLE.

Further Particulars.

The Survivors Rescued After Ten Hours.

Heartrending Scenes.

(By Electric Telegraph—Copyright.)

(Per United Press Association.)

LONDON, June 19.

Mr Currie, one of the owners of the Drummond Castle, attributes the disaster to a haze.

The captain and officers were on the bridge at the time of the accident, and no light could be seen.

For two hours previous to striking the fog horn sounded.

Twenty-five bodies have been recovered.

The Queen has sent a message to the company expressing her deep distress at the accident.

When the Drummond Castle struck it was raining and dark, and most of the adult passengers were on deck. There was a grating sound when the steamer struck, and the officers at once ordered the boats to be lowered, but before they could be launched the vessel sank bow foremost. The seamen who survived clung to a basket and a plank, and drifted about for ten hours before being rescued by fishermen. The air was filled with shrieks by those struggling for life, for several minutes after the accident happened. Among those drowned were several women and children, and one family of 16. Ten naval officers were among the passengers.

The newspaper article describing the accident.

Right: Newspaper drawing of the courageous people trying to rescue victims.

Previous page: Beautiful image of the wreck. The size of the diver gives you an idea of the dimensions of the huge propeller.

It was busy in the port of Cape Town on 28th May 1896 as the passenger liner *Drummond Castle* was being made ready to set sail for London. The deck officers presented a final report to Captain Pierce, who then gave the order to cast off. The voyage went well, and during a stopover in Las Palmas fresh food and coal were taken on board. Throughout the journey the 143 passengers were entertained by the more than 100 crew members who served on board the luxury liner. On 16th June the *Drummond Castle* passed the island of Ushant (Ouessant in French) off the coast of Brittany, a day's sailing from her home port. This area had a reputation for being one of the most treacherous places in the world to navigate, with more than forty-two ships sunk there in the previous twenty years. Although mighty storms were not uncommon here, this was a calm night but with limited visibility due to fog. Captain Pierce had no idea that his ship was 5 miles off course due to localised strong currents, or that it was heading straight towards the cliffs. Between 22:00 and 23:00 the *Drummond Castle* was seen by the watch of the steamer *Werfer*, who noticed that she was sailing too close to shore. Around midnight the liner rammed the Pierres Vertes (Green Cliffs) near the Fromveur Sound at full speed. The captain, thinking the ship was stuck on the rocks, did not give the order to lower the lifeboats.

However, the ship immediately came free of the rocks and within four minutes she sank to the bottom. The speed of the sinking caught almost all the passengers off guard, and as a result most drowned. The only surviving passenger was Charlie Marquardt, who was able to grab on to some driftwood and was rescued by

A museum in Molene has numerous remainders of the ship.

The grave of Englishman Herbert Hinds, thirty-one years old and crew member of the *Drummond Castle*.

The island of Molene, Brittany.

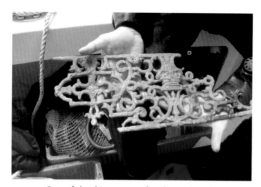

Part of the décor, very refined metal work.

Shipping company logo on a plate.

Crystal whisky
carafe.

Wine decanter
with logo.

fisherman Joseph Berthele, from the island of Molene. Berthele was a retired fisherman who, immediately after the disaster, sailed to the area in his small boat. Apart from Charlie, he also recovered the body of four-year-old Alice Reid from the cold seawater. Two crew members, supply officer Charles Wood and sailor William Godbolt, were able to save themselves by clinging on to driftwood, and were later rescued by some local fishermen. The year 1996 was the first centennial of the shipwrecking, and the people from the island organised a large memorial service at the site of the disaster.

DIVE INTO THE PAST

Many years ago I was reading the book *Het goud van de Egypt* (*The Gold of Egypt*), and a short chapter was devoted to diving the wreck of the *Drummond Castle*, as the Italian salvage company Sorima had been active on it for a brief period during the 1930s. The book described the fierce currents at the site that make diving nearly impossible. The following spring I met Gilbert, a local diver from the Brest area who had a boat and a diving centre and was willing to take us to the wreck. Gilbert was born on the island of Ushant and knew the local waters like the back of this hand. This was very important because circumstances make diving the wreck possible on only a couple of occasions each year. It is only possible during slack tide and even then there should not be too much swell in order to get out to the ship.

So it was with little hope that our team left Belgium in the spring of 2009 to try to dive the *Drummond Castle* and capture some photos of her. For a base of operations we had rented a house close to the dive centre. Here we had enough room for the eight members of this expedition, and there was also room for blending our diving gases.

Each morning after breakfast we drove from our base to the dive centre in order to get our gear ready. To get into the swing of things, on the first day we dived a wreck that was a little bit shallower and closer to shore. The *Saracen* is a freighter that was sunk during the Second World War, and she lies on the seabed at a depth of 56m. The dive went well, with visibility of at least 10m; the wreck was still nicely intact, sitting upright on the seabed. After the dive the gear and rebreathers were prepared for the next day's attempt to dive the *Drummond Castle*. The weather report remained favourable so it was a matter of trying now or having to wait a year for another opportunity.

FIRST SURVEY OF THE WRECK

The next day, when we met up at 09:00 at the dive centre everyone was a little on edge. Due to all kinds of external factors, a wreck dive in an area like this could, regardless of all the preparations, still go wrong at the last minute. The trip out to the wreck was nevertheless smooth, and soon it was time for the first team to get ready to hit the water. On Gilbert's recommendation, we waited another ten minutes for the current to disappear altogether. Karl van der Auwera and I jumped into the water as the second team and immediately started to swim for the buoy to start our descent along the shot line. It took us four minutes to descend the 65m to the wreck, and once there we took time to get our bearings. The visibility was still pretty decent but it was dark at depth. We couldn't immediately work out where on the wreck we had landed so we started to swim in a southerly direction, all the time unrolling our reels. It didn't take long until we saw the first portholes, still in the plates of the hull. A bit further on I discovered the remnants of the bridge telegraph, which was an indication that we were on the middle of the wreck. Continuing on, we saw two of the boilers in the sand, which were still intact, and in their vicinity were several part of the steam engine. The bollards, which were used to moor the ship, were also still clearly recognisable. We quickly ran out of our planned twenty minutes of bottom time and had to hurry to send up our DSMB decompression markers to start our decompression. After about ninety minutes we were picked up by Gilbert and greeted by members of the other teams who were already on board. Everyone agreed that it had been a magnificent dive and that we should definitely return to this wreck.

EXPEDITION 2000

One year later we returned to Brittany to dive the wreck again. This time the weather gods weren't smiling down on us and there was a heavy swell. Gilbert was a skipper who could flawlessly judge the conditions on different wrecks, and after some consulting we headed out to the *Drummond Castle*. The trip wasn't very smooth, and we were well shaken by the time we arrived on site. Once we had the shot line on the wreck it was a matter of getting into our gear and jumping into the water as quickly as possible. At a depth of 10m the swell disappeared and we could take

Brass/copper steam pipes of the boilers.

Boiler.

Port hole in hull.

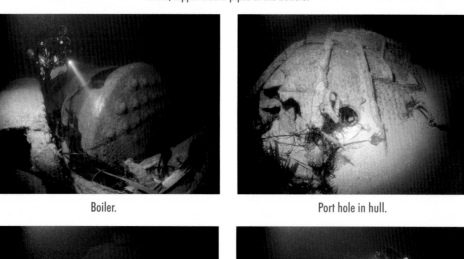

Mast support.

Bollards.

Left: The ship's telegraph.
Above: The dive team.

our time to acclimatise and to do the necessary checks. The visibility on the wreck was better than the previous time, and at a depth of 65m there was still plenty of daylight.

Almost immediately we saw one of the giant bronze propellers still on the propeller shaft – we were on the stern section of the wreck. Following the direction of the propeller shaft we again saw the hull plates that had opened outward. The portholes in the hull were clearly recognisable in some places. We also came across one of the mast standing rigging supports still attached to the capping rail. The mast itself was nowhere to be seen; it had probably broken off on collision with the cliffs. For the second time we could now clearly make out the boilers and many surrounding brass/copper steam pipes.

In this area we also found porcelain with the logo of the shipping company, indicating that the galley wasn't far away. Then it was time once again to start our ascent, a time to sharpen all of one's senses so as not to make a mistake. A free ascent after a bottom time of nearly twenty-five minutes at a depth of 65m had to be executed accurately and according to the dive plan. There was no room for error – the penalties could be severe. After signalling my buddy, we first ascended 15m and then we deployed our DSMBs. This is when the long wait started during the many stages of our decompression profile. Back on the boat there was plenty of time to swap dive stories, but everyone was in agreement that the *Drummond Castle* was a nice wreck with a beautiful history.

SS *LEOPOLDVILLE*

THE CONGO BOAT TORPEDOED

When the Belgian troop transport ship SS *Leopoldville* was torpedoed, 763 young American soldiers died. It was the largest American loss of servicemen at sea in a single action during the Second World War. In the interests of American morale, the military censors ordered the survivors to keep the tragedy secret. Only long after the end of the war did the truth of what really happened come to light.

SS *Leopoldville*

Type: Passenger ship
Built: John Cockerill Hoboken, 1929
Owner: Compagnie Maritime Belge
Tonnage: 11,509 tons
Dimensions: Length 165m, beam 11.5m
Speed: 16 Knots

A huge crowd shows up to see the launch.

Above: Slowly the *Leopoldville* slides into the river Schelde.
Previous page: The cannon is clearly recognisable.

Queen Astrid and King Leopold III show a lot of interest in this luxury cruiseship.

A FLOATING PALACE

When the passenger ship *Leopoldville* was launched in 1927 at the shipyard John Cockerill in Hoboken near Antwerp, it immediately entered into service on the Antwerp–Matadi line.

The Compagnie Belge Maritime du Congo used it to transport passengers and goods to the Belgian Congo – so the ship was soon nicknamed 'the Congo boat'. She was, however, also used as a luxury cruise liner to other destinations, including Norway, Morocco and Algeria. On these trips, the rich passengers were treated to the seldom seen luxury of the beautiful art deco interior in this floating palace.

Every effort was taken to make the trip unforgettable for the passengers. The meals were prepared with utmost attention, and every day people could choose from different menus. For entertainment, there was a library, a gym and a swimming pool, and all kinds of activities were organised for the passengers.

In the first class cabins, the passengers had their own cabin boy. These cabin boys were mainly Congolese, and had separate quarters to eat and sleep. When the Second World War broke out, the ship was immediately chartered by the British Admiralty as a troop transport. After a series of adaptations and necessary armament, the *Leopoldville* took on its new task. From May 1940 to December 1944 more than 120,000 troops were transported and 219,949 miles sailed without incident.

CHRISTMAS EVE 1944

On 24th December 1944 at 09:00 the *Leopoldville* left Southampton, England, to take 2,235 American soldiers of the 66th Infantry Division to Cherbourg, France. These soldiers were mobilised to stop the Von Rundstedt campaign in the Belgian Ardennes. When they cast off, a harsh breeze of Beaufort force 6 blew from the south-west. It was very cold and the trip was uncomfortable. When they approached the French coast, Captain Charles Limbor gave the order to the first officer to sail in a zig-zag pattern, as there had been a warning from one of the three accompanying destroyers about the potential for a U-boat attack. Roughly 5 miles out from the entrance to the Port of Cherbourg, the German submarine U-486 was awaiting its prey. Captained by Oblt Gerhard Meyer, it was equipped with a new snorkel device that enabled it to stay underwater while charging its batteries. When evening had fallen, Meyer spotted the *Leopoldville*, attacked and fired a torpedo that hit her on the starboard side. The explosion was enormous.

THE RESCUE OPERATION

Immediately, an SOS was sent out and several ships came to the rescue, including a tugboat, but they couldn't do anything since Captain Limbor had dropped anchor to avoid the ship floating into a minefield. Commander Pringle of the British destroyer HMS *Brilliant* brought his ship alongside in an effort to save more lives, but sadly many were still lost.

The departure from Antwerp.

Goodbye for a long time.

On the quay..

A game of ability.

A game of tug-of-war.

Dessert buffet..

Gramophone.

Swimming pool.

The captain posing with two passengers.

For medical care there was a nurse aboard.

Luggage on deck.

A happy passenger with a
Leopoldville ribbon.

Promenade deck.

The *Leopoldville* at anchor in a foreign port.

Many jumped too early or too late, thus falling between the two ships in the ice cold water. Many wounded who were tied on to stretchers also fell between the two ships and drowned. For those in the water, their chances of survival were slim due to the temperature and choppiness of the water. Some 763 soldiers died in this catastrophe; among them were twins from New York, Clarence and Carl Carlson whose bodies were never found. Private Angelo Catalano died on his twenty-first birthday, and his body was also never found. His brother, Jerry, later testified as to how difficult it was for the family to celebrate Christmas in the years following the tragedy.

The Supreme Command of the Allied Forces tried to keep details of the loss secret and it was only in 1996 that the British Admiralty released documents that revealed what really occurred that night. Since then, a monument has been raised for the victims in Fort Benning Georgia, USA. Under the direction of Allan Andrade, the survivors meet every year to commemorate their fallen comrades. Allan is a retired police officer from New York who made the tragedy public. He also published a book with testimonies of survivors and their families.

At the 2006 gathering, my diving buddy Danny Huyghe filmed some very moving testimonies for the documentary he was making about the torpedoing of the *Leopoldville*.

DIVING ON THE *LEOPOLDVILLE*

The wreck of the *Leopoldville* is situated only 5 miles from the port of Cherbourg but lies at a depth of 60m. Dennis Leonard and Jean Olive of the French Naval Diving Team accompanied us. They acquired all the necessary permits to dive on this official war grave. Not wanting to waste precious diving time, each phase of the dive was carefully planned and the blueprints of the ship were studied meticulously.

After a speedy descent, we landed on the starboard side of the wreck. Immediately, we swam over the edge to the deck in the direction of the bow gun. I took several pictures here and we continued swimming to the middle of the wreck. It was amazing that the deck planks were still there after so many years, as well as the big winches to load the ship. The visibility was at least 8m.

When we returned to the upper part of the wreck, I saw in one of the aisles a stack of helmets and a pile of ammunition that had been left behind when the soldiers jumped overboard. After a few more pictures, our twenty-two minutes of diving time had passed and we had to start our decompression. The intense dive and the incredible condition of the ship were overwhelming, and we had a lively conversation about it once we were back on the boat. Unfortunately, the wind gained strength and the dive for the next day was cancelled. We had to start our return trip of 650km to Belgium but we vowed to come back in 2006.

FURTHER EXPLORATION OF THE WRECK

In September 2006 we planned two consecutive trips to the wreck. We would dive with Trimix to considerably extend our diving time to forty minutes at 57m. This

A document listing the contents of the safe.

First mate Henri Gubel.

The twins Clarence and Carl Carlson from New York did not survived the attack.

Publicity to promote the African route.

A menu on the crossing to the USA.

Jozef Tibodeau.

The grave of Jozef Tibodeau.

also meant that the dive itself became much more complex. The two gas switches during ascent on a reel, with a huge camera, gave me quite a bit of stress. During this dive, team member Danny Huyghe captured some video.

We landed at approximately the same spot as the previous year, and proceeded immediately to the centre and over the edge into the depths. Again we passed by the huge winches and part of the superstructure. Then we saw an enormous hole where the torpedo had hit the ship; it is impressive to see the damage that 250kg of TNT can inflict. We swam into the wreck and saw the shoes, rifles, Sten guns and closed backpacks of the fallen soldiers. The scene was emotional, and made me reflect on the young lives that were lost here.

The survivors in front of the monument erected for the victims in fort Benning, Georgia, USA.

Allan Andrade, a retired New York police officer, organises the reunions in memory of their fallen friends.

The liferafts could have saved many lives.

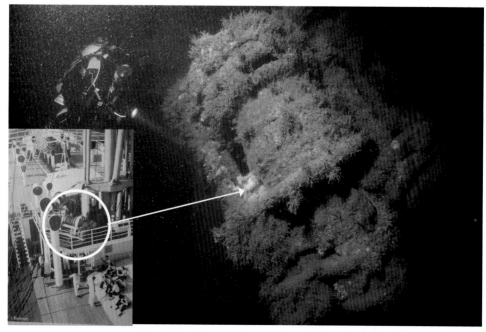

Winch.

Terrible weather conditions on the way out to the wreck.

Breathing gas cylinders filled with
trimix are brought aboard.

When we left Cherbourg port the next day, a strong wind was blowing and it increased in force the farther we travelled from shore. When we arrived at the wreck site, it was clear that diving under these circumstances was out of the question, so we had to return to the harbour.

ENTRANCE IN TO THE MACHINE ROOM

Two weeks later we dived the wreck again to take a closer look at the torpedo hole.

Just before the spot where the ship was broken, I discovered several large objects on the starboard side. These items turned out to be three life rafts, which must have been tied to the ship when disaster struck, otherwise they would have floated away.

I took a few photos and swam to the stern. We were at a depth of 57m and I decided to enter the wreck with my diving buddy Eric Wouters. We did so where the engine room was situated. We went into a narrow aisle and had to turn right. Eric attached his reel to make sure we could find our way out, as it was too risky to lose our sense of direction. We could see clearly the cranes and pipes that one can expect in an engine room. The passage was very narrow and we experienced difficulty manoeuvring. We continued swimming and came into another room, where we saw several running frames. Then we signalled each other that it had become too dangerous to proceed, and it was time to start our ascent. Back on board, we discussed the discovery of the life rafts with our French colleagues. It turned out that they had never noticed them before, and they were really surprised when we told them where they were. The next day, we shot video footage of the rafts, which were a very important part of the whole picture as they could have saved dozens of lives if they had been used. The survivors told us later that they couldn't untie them because the knots were frozen.

A gas mask, proof of the military task of the *Leopoldville*.

A WRECK THAT DOESN'T LEAVE YOU UNTOUCHED

The *Leopoldville* tragedy is something that will always stay in my mind, and I think that is the case for all the different team members with whom I have dived on the wreck. The stories of the young soldiers that left for a foreign country to save it from Nazism have really touched me.

After the war, there were bitter discussions about the Belgian crew, who were blamed for not having done enough to save the soldiers. I think that in this type of disaster, the overall panic is bound to lead to casualties. Silent witnesses of this are the military life rafts that are still there!

Storeroom.

Lifeboat davits.

Bottles of beer.

Portholes.

Square porthole.

Entrance door.

Divers penetrating the wreck.

Shoes lying as silent witnesses of the victims.

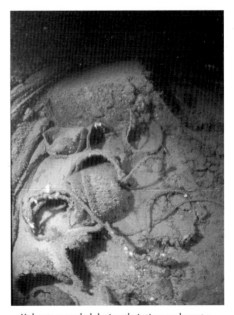

Helmets corroded during their time underwater.

SS *ALBERTVILLE*

A LUXURY MAIL SHIP SINKS

The air raid was not unexpected; however the
howling sirens of the Stuka dive bombers still took
the crew of the SS *Albertville* by surprise.

SS Albertville

Type: Passenger ship/troop transport
Built: Ateliers et chantiers de la Loire/St-Naraire, France, 1928
Shipping company: Compagnie Maritime Belge
Propulsion: Turbine/screw
Tonnage: 10,269 tons
Dimensions: Length 153m, beam 19.15m

Hostesses always smiling!

The Compagnie Maritime Belge, founded in 1895, is one of Antwerp's oldest shipping companies. Under the influence of King Leopold II of Belgium, and with the help of British investors, a permanent connection was established with the King's Belgian Congo state. For more than sixty years many missionaries, civil servants and adventurers made use of the 'Congo ships' to travel to this Belgian

Publicity posters

colony; on return trips valuable cargos were often carried, such as diamonds, ivory and rubber. The Compagnie Maritime Belge then commissioned the building of a new ship to allow it to offer trips to this remote part of Africa.

The order went to a French shipyard in the port city of Saint-Nazaire – the ship would be built in such a way that it was also able to be used as a cruiseliner. The interior was sumptuous, designed in the art deco style that was considered modern at the time. When the ship was delivered in 1928 it could reach a speed of 15 knots, which was a satisfactory result for a ship of its type. The *Albertville* was immediately deployed on the Africa line to carry goods and people on a fixed schedule to the port of Matadi. At that time even locomotives and railway carriages were shipped to the Congo.

The ship was also used on a few successful cruises to, among others, America and Africa. However, as the competition from other shipping companies was increasing, the CMB board of directors decided in 1936 to refurbish the ship at the Mercantile Marine Engineering & Graving Dock Co. NV of Antwerp. The old steam engines were replaced by turbine engines that enabled the *Albertville* to sail 2 knots faster. The two smoke stacks were replaced by a single one and the ship was lengthened by 7m. The entire interior was completely refurbished – including an extensively equipped gym.

During cruises the emphasis was placed on luxury and an impeccable service. The food was of an extraordinary quality and available in large quantities; the galleys were equipped with new and modern equipment. Every day a new menu was prepared by the chef, printed on board and distributed among the passengers. A reading room, a chapel and a children's nursery were also available.

THE WAR YEARS

The ship was being used on cruises when the first signs of war became apparent. When Belgium became involved in the fighting, the government fled to England, where it continued to govern in exile. In the meantime, the SS *Albertville* was impressed by the military and equipped with rapid fire guns and a 75mm cannon, with the white hull repainted grey. Some weeks later, in May 1940, the ship was used during the evacuation of troops from the besieged Dunkirk, where almost 400,000 Allied soldiers were trapped by German troops; the invaluable SS *Albertville* was able to transport thousands of soldiers to England.

The *Albertville* at full steam.

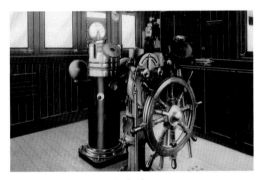

The bridge.

A lifeboat.

During her next mission the ship was sent to Le Havre to help with the evacuation of the city. Le Havre was heavily bombarded and the oil depots were burning. When the SS *Albertville* tried to enter the port she was denied access as the docks were full with other ships. Together with the passenger ship SS *Général Metzinger*, the SS *Albertville* waited several miles outside the port to come into action and take on board the troops.

On 11th June 1940 the SS *Albertville* was attacked by Stuka dive bombers – a few large bombs landed barely 4m from the ship. The glass of the portholes could not withstand the pressure of the near misses and shattered, allowing water to rush in. The captain ordered the anchor to be raised and directed the ship closer to shore, where it was protected by the coastal batteries and enjoyed more protection than at sea. The German pilots, however, would not leave their prey, and the ship

A souvenir picture

The promenade deck.

The staircase.

The kitchen.

On the quay..

suffered several direct hits. The engines and the radio equipment were disabled, and to make matters worse the hull fractured below the waterline. The SS *Albertville* took on a 30 degree list and the captain gave the order to lower the lifeboats and abandon ship. She sank thirty minutes later without a single casualty.

A FORGOTTEN SHIPWRECK

In the following years the wreck of the SS *Albertville* was completely forgotten about; with only divers from a local club making the occasional dive on it. The wreck lies close to the port entrance of the busy port of Le Havre, and the visibility is usually limited. This is why the Paul Eluard Dive Club rarely visits the wreck, so when I made plans with my buddy Stefan Panis to dive it we were lucky to receive its help.

Since the trip to the wreck is a short one, we prepared our rebreathers on the shore before loading them on to the boat. As such, we could immediately start

Above: The expedition ship of diving club Paul Eluard.

Left: A bottle of wine.

getting geared up when we arrived at the wreck site. After a quarter of an hour's preparation, we were ready to board the dive club boat. On the radio we listened to the latest weather forecast – only a little wind was predicted, and the sea was calm when we left the port.

The captain on duty had no problems finding the wreck, and an anchor with a buoy was dropped over the side when we passed over it. The first dive team to jump in the water had to check if the anchor was positioned correctly on the wreck. We waited several minutes and then jumped overboard. While descending the visibility was only about 1m, and it was clear this was not going to be an easy dive.

Above: Winch clearly recognisable.

Left: Stefan and Vic, ready to splash.

Bronzen letters

The ship's bell, a symbolic find.

Brass letters of the ship's name.

A CAUTIOUS JOURNEY

We quickly found out that we were on the starboard side of the ship. The wreck was at an angle of 30 degrees on a sandy bottom. This sand was churned up by the current and this caused the bad visibility. We did not let this distract us and followed the hull of the ship, finding many portholes still attached to the hull, some of them only hanging by a single bolt. Still, here in France the wrecks are protected as heritage sites, and look but don't touch is the message.

The visibility on the upper part of the wreck could be called fair, about 2m, but gradually became worse the deeper we swam. We found ourselves on the deck and noticed one of the hatches to the hold below. Here the visibility was barely 1m, and we cautiously swam onwards, being careful not to get entangled in fishing nets. Beyond the hatch of the cargo hold, the wreck was covered by sand and we returned to the topside. An electric motor was partially hidden and it was clear we were now swimming between different parts of the engine room. Lots of fishing lines were present on the wreck, which hindered us greatly; we had to free ourselves numerous times when our equipment got caught.

After forty minutes we decided to return to the down line, but at the same time the current became noticeably stronger and the visibility decreased even further. It took us more than twenty minutes to start ascending. After more than an hour of diving we finally returned on board and the anchor was lifted.

Stefan and Vic: focused before the dive, relaxed after.

EXPLORATION OF THE FORECASTLE

Several months later we returned to Le Havre to make a second dive on the wreck. By coincidence we anchored on almost exactly the same spot, but this time we decided to head in the direction of the forecastle. After a few minutes my buddy, Stefan Panis, found an empty wine bottle in the wreckage. Lots of pieces of broken pots were found in this area, which led us to believe we might be in the vicinity of the storage holds.

The visibility was again about 1.5m, but with little current we made good progress. Suddenly, we saw a huge windlass in front of us, which most likely served the cargo booms on the deck. I took several pictures of this, which was in reasonable condition and easily recognisable. We now swam back closer to the sandy bottom and the sand immediately started to swirl, so we swam to a higher part of the wreck to experience less trouble with the sediment. We returned to the starboard side and recognised some bronze portholes.

The edge of the ship now curved inwards, and we discovered large brass letters that were barely attached to the wreck. They appeared to be the letters T and V; we were now at the tip of the clearly discernible bow. As I was taking pictures here Stefan made me aware it was time to return to the surface. We had now spent more than an hour on the bottom and still had to travel a large distance to the downline, which was somewhere in the middle of the wreck. Stefan now swam ahead of me because he was reeling in the thin guideline we had laid out. During this I had to pay attention not to lose sight of him, because I would then have no way of finding my way back to the downline. Everything went well, and on the way back we even had time to appreciate some of the lifeboat davits. Our dive time was now beyond an hour and a half, and reluctantly we left the wreck behind us; there was much more still to discover on this wreck than we had seen. Back on board we discussed our dive and agreed that we should return soon to make further explorations of the wreck.

THE FRIGATE *LUTINE*

THE GOLDEN TREASURE OF THE TORMENTOR

In 1799 the *Lutine* (tormentor) perished in a
heavy storm off the coast of the Vlieland island.
Due to her large cargo of gold, 200 years later
she is still a target for treasure hunters.

Lutine

Type: Armoured frigate
Built: Toulon, France
Owner: Royal Navy
Propulsion: Sails
Tonnage: 1,100 tons
Dimensions: Length 45m, beam 11.5m
Speed: 11 knots

The treasure caught the attention of the newspapers!
Previos page: Cannons and cannon balls on an eighteenth century shipwreck.

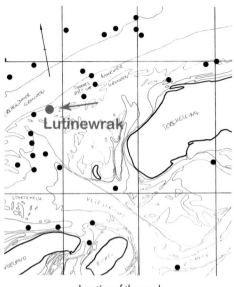

Location of the wreck.

Thirty-three-year-old Captain Lancelot Skinner was quite inexperienced at sailing the waters around Vlieland when the *Lutine* found herself in a heavy storm. It was 9th October 1799, and the first winter storm of the year was raging with all its might. The entire crew was hard at work trying to save the ship, which was carrying a cargo of 1,920kg of gold and 2,000kg of silver. During the storm the helmsman made a navigational error and unexpectedly ended up in between treacherous sandbanks in the North Sea.

The Razende Bol is a sandbank that had already claimed numerous ships, and now it had the *Lutine* in its grip. The ship, built at a shipyard in Toulon, at first resisted her fate but eventually gave up and sank. Only one of the 280 crew reached the shore alive. The islands of Vlieland and Terschelling were occupied by the British at that time and they immediately dispatched a ship to safeguard the treasure against plundering. People then did not pay too much attention to the rule of law, and the islanders were true beachcombers who took anything that washed ashore as their property. Rumours quickly went around that part of the cargo was recovered before the British arrived.

THE ISLANDERS TAKE THEIR CHANCE

When the British occupation force left in 1800, the true salvage attempts to recover the gold started. The cargo was insured through Lloyd's of London, and it stood to recover a large part of the proceeds when the treasure was recovered, although there would still be enough left over for a salvor to finance an expedition and get rich. During the first salvage operations, crane grabs rather than divers were used, as they could pick the small barrels of gold from the wreck. In calm weather, when the water was clear, the salvors could see the cannonballs on the deck of the wreck. By 1801, 500,000 Euros worth of gold and silver had been recovered in this manner.

However, the wreck disappeared underneath the North Sea sand, and it was not until 1821 that another attempt could be made. Mayor Eschauzier of Terschelling was interested in the treasure and wanted to use a diving bell. The caisson was open on the underside and four people could work on the seabed at the same time. However, the North Sea is not an ideal place in which to work with diving equipment as the current and bad visibility hamper proceedings. This work therefore failed, and the attempts were stopped after one season.

Salvaged cannon.

A carronade.

Above and right: Engraving of hard hat divers working at a wreck site.

Coins.

Spanish coins.

THE FIRST HELMET DIVERS ENTER THE WRECK

When the brass diving helmet with direct air supply from the surface was invented in 1828, there was a fresh chance to salvage the gold, as divers could now work for hours underwater. In 1834, one of the Deane brothers dived to the wreck several times and one dive even lasted for more than two hours. However, not a single gram of gold was recovered, so the Deane brothers also abandoned their attempt.

In 1857 a new salvage company was started in the Netherlands that worked with helmet divers. It had more success and succeeded in salvaging forty-one gold bars. This success brought other rivals, and the salvors had to call in the help of a government gunboat to protect them.

Archive pictures of the *Lyons*.

The gold-seeking tower.

The Beckers tower in full action.

Frans Beckers and his associates.

Besides the gold bars the divers found sixty-four silver ingots and 15,300 gold and silver coins. The bell of the *Lutine* was also found and handed over to Lloyd's. It was left in a dusty office and forgotten about until it resurfaced later and was placed in the hall of the Lloyd's building, where it still is today. The bell is tolled once when bad news is announced (for example a sinking) and twice when it is good news.

THE ENGLISH ARRIVE AND MAKE A SECOND ATTEMPT

In 1910 a new company was set up in England to make a fresh attempt on the wreck. The British National Salvage Association raised enough money and equipped the former ferry *Lyons* for this salvage. Captain Gardiner was in charge of the operation and had much experience in salvage. With a crew of forty-five men plus ten experienced divers, the party was convinced it had a good chance of getting to the wreck and the treasure. However, due to bad luck with the equipment, it was not until January 1911 that the team started airlifting the sand above the wreck site. During the first weeks many wreck pieces and two anchors were recovered from the ship. The discovery of a lot of cannonballs gave the salvors hope that they would find gold. Unfortunately, when the First World War broke out the project was stopped by the British, and they quietly left the island. The time of the British salvors was now definitely over.

The *Karimata*.

English divers.

Kelly Tarlton and John Neuschwander.

Irwien.

THE GOLD-SEARCHER'S TOWER OF FRANS BECKERS

In January 1938 local newspapers reported that businessman Frans Beckers from Gennep had come up with a daring plan to retrieve the gold from the wreck: Beckers wanted to build a tower that could be submerged above the wreck. The shipping company Doeksen & Dros promptly secured the contract. The plans showed the tower to have a diameter of 12m on the bottom and 3m at the top. Once submerged above the wreck, it could be emptied of water and the divers would be able to work in dry conditions. The tower was equipped with light and a ventilation system to supply the divers with fresh air.

The big advantage of this invention would be that divers could work for more days on the wreck without depending on the visibility under water. Shares in the project were sold to whoever was interested. On 27th May 1933 the tower was ready and the pumps were tested. On 21st July the tower was brought outside by a tugboat and positioned above the wreck. Up until that moment all was perfect. But then the weather deteriorated and the crew could not reach the tower for days. When they returned on 26th August the tower was heavily damaged by the weather. However, Beckers had a new, stronger tower made in the winter of 1933–34. Cannonballs and pieces of wreckage were salvaged, but no more substantial progress was made. After an accident that caused the death of a diver, this attempt was also abandoned. The whole operation recovered just one single gold coin.

THE LARGEST TIN MINING DREDGER IS A MARVEL

In 1938 at Smit shipyard in Kinderdijk the finishing touches were completed to the tin mining dredger *Karimata*. Its owner, the mining company Billiton, aimed to use this vessel in Indonesia to dig for tin. The *Karimata* was 75m long, had a beam of 23m and could move 400 cu m of soil in an hour, making it the largest tin mining dredger in the world. As the tow out to the Dutch East Indies was planned for July or August, it would lie idle for a few months in port.

Billiton therefore decided it could be used to attempt to raise the gold, and research immediately started into the currents and seabed around the wreck site. After another contract was signed with the shipping company Doeksen, the *Karimata* left Kinderdijk for Terschelling on 4th June 1938. The *Karimata* was moored above the wreck by 40mm thick cables, so as to be able to work during bad weather. On 9th June the first buckets were dredged. Several silver and copper coins were found but not much else.

On 29 July, a gold bar of 3.5kg was finally dredged to the surface, which convinced everyone that the rest of the treasure would be found quickly. Even at Lloyd's the news was well received and the bell of the *Lutine* was tolled twice. The salvors continued searching around the location of the first gold bar but found nothing besides one gold coin and several iron cannon. On 12th September the Billiton Company ceased its work at the site. Its salvage attempt had been the most expensive one at the wreck so far, costing it 450,000 guilders.

Salvage vessel *Yak*.

Grave of Captain Skinner on the island Vlieland.

NEW ZEALANDERS ARE STRUCK BY GOLD FEVER

In the 1980s a team led by Kelly Tarlton dived the wreck from its ship *Yak*. Tarlton was a treasure hunter in heart and soul, and earned his spurs by locating the Rothschild Diamonds in the hulk of the *Tasmania*, which was wrecked off the shores of Australia in 1897. He also worked with Robert Marx, one of the most famous wreck divers in the world.

FIFTEENTH SEARCH FOR GOLD

Dentist Arne Duif from Harlingen had been preoccupied with the treasure since 1989, and, together with a dive team called Caranan, tried to find information about the location of the wreck in a scientific way. Duif was not specifically interested in the gold but wanted to reconstruct the full story of the sinking. Therefore, he worked with the company Metaldec International BV, which lent him a special sonar device. He was the first individual to have an agreement with Lloyd's to work on the wreck site; as it was also protected under heritage law, an agreement was also made with the Netherlands Institute for Ship and Underwater Archaeology (NISA).

According to Duif's theory, the stern of the ship, along with a large part of the gold cargo, had drifted from its original location. As yet he has still not found any gold, with the most recent newspaper article about the operation being written in 2002.

TOMBSTONE FOR CAPTAIN SKINNER

In the 1980s a tombstone was raised on Vlieland in memory of Captain Skinner of the *Lutine*. The memorial was made according to an old English design and largely paid for by Lloyd's, which still owns the salvage rights. With this gesture respect was paid by the people of the island to the captain of this unfortunate ship. During the different salvage attempts it was learned that his ship had broken in two and was a total loss.

THE MS *CHRISTIAAN HUYGENS*

ART TREASURES FROM A SHIPWRECK

In 1927 the motor ship *Christiaan Huygens* became the largest passenger ship ever built in the Netherlands. Furnished by the famous designer Lion Cachet, it was finished in expensive materials such as marble and mahogany. The luxury passenger ship was badly damaged by a mine at the end of the Second World War and became a total loss.

MS Christiaan Huygens

Type: passenger ship
Built: Nederlandse scheepsbouwmaatschappij, Amsterdam
Owner: Stoomvaart maatschappij Nederland
Launched: 28 september 1928
Propulsion: Turbine, 1 propeller
Tonnage: 16,280 tons
Dimensions: Length 168m, beam 21m

Tug boat offers help to the sinking ship

Above: The launching of this graceful ship.
Bottom left: The ship sitting broken on the bank after the heavy explosion.
Previous page: The port side cannon in front of the bridge
Inset: Shells (grenades) stored beneath the cannon

ANTWERP 1945

On 25th August the MS *Huygens* left the port of Antwerp destined for Rotterdam. The weather was good, with just a light breeze of Beaufort force 3. Shortly into the voyage the pilot was exchanged off Terneuzen. At 20:49 Captain Bakker gave the order to drop anchor in order for the ship to spend the night in the vicinity of buoy No. 3. On Sunday morning at around 06:00 the anchor was raised and the captain ordered the voyage resumed. When the MS *Huygens* passed the wreck buoy of the *Empire Blessing* at around 07:56 the officer of the watch reported in the deck logbook that all was in order.

However, a few hours later, at 11:30, a large explosion took place. Immediately, all engines were stopped and the captain ordered an emergency distress message to be sent. The lifeboats were made ready to offload the passengers, several of whom were wounded by the explosion. The captain signalled the tugboat *Arthur* to come alongside as soon as possible – while all the time, water rushed into the cargo holds.

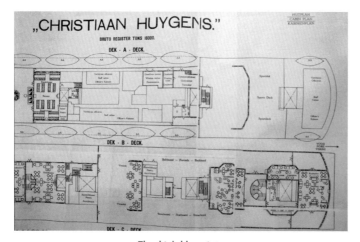

The ship's blueprint.

Sculptor Lambertus Zijl.

Beautiful art deco statue.
Above: How it was found.

After preservation.

At 15:30 Captain Bakker held a meeting with his senior officers, and it was decided to beach the ship on a sandbank 4 miles away so it could be salvaged at a later time. The ship was taken in tow towards the sand bank and beached. In the following days several attempts were made to save the ship, but unfortunately a heavy storm came through and broke it in two. On 3rd September the ship was written off as a total loss.

Attempts were made to save as much as possible from the ship; the compasses, telegraphs, radio equipment and binoculars. Even the table silver that could be reached was saved from perishing. Throughout the years the ship sank deeper and deeper in the North Sea and was finally lost into oblivion.

A DIVE INTO THE UNKNOWN

When I made my first dive on the wreck of the *Christiaan Huygens* on 29th May 1991 I could not have imagined that this wreck would still keep me captivated many years later. However, the first dive was not a success. We did not have any GPS navigation systems, and it was a challenge to find the wreck with just a compass and a map. However, we got lucky when we followed several buoys as a small day fisher was anchored on the wreck. Quickly, we threw the anchor and prepared ourselves to explore.

While descending along the shot line I could feel a very strong current and the visibility was reduced to nil. I decided to detach the anchor and we called it a day. We did not give up though, and we returned to the wreck many times that season. We found the visibility under water was better on some days than others, and we slowly got to know the wreck.

THE FIRST BRONZE STATUES

During the season of 1992 we again dived on the wreck regularly. One day in July, at a depth of 20m, my curiosity was triggered by a bronze ring sticking out of the sand. Using my dive knife to clear it away, a figure featuring three naked women appeared. As I dug deeper a beautiful bronze statue became visible. Back on the boat, the find was studied and we figured it was most likely a lamp foot. I had left my reel next to my find, and shortly afterwards my buddy found a statue of a cat close by. Several weeks later we also found a statue of an owl. Other objects such as silver dishes and porcelain were also found at different spots. In the following years I made many dives at the site, even though I prioritised other wrecks.

RESEARCH IN THE ARCHIVE

In 1999 I had a bit more time on my hands, so after a tip-off I started researching in the National Archives in The Hague. Here I found a booklet with pictures of the various compartments of the ship and a description of the interior. This document identified the bronze statues that were used in the first class dining hall; they were

Aquarelles showing the stylish interiors of the ship.

Children's room.

Reading room.

Luxury cabin.

Promenade deck.

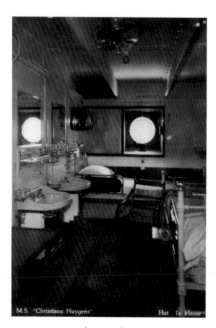

A luxury cabin.

easily recognisable as the ones we had found. The bronze statue with the three naked ladies was placed on an ebony wooden side table along the wall, and there was also a second statue.

In between the statues, a tapestry hung with a representation of Paris in the time of Christiaan Huygens. The statues were made by the famous Dutch sculptor Lambertus Zijl on Cachet's orders. The interior decoration and sculptures were designed in the contemporary art deco style. This art form originated from Paris during the early 1920s and distinguished itself by clean lines in the design.

In a different archive I even found the original order form for the casting of the statues at the Belgian foundry Fonderie Nationales des Bronzes. The statues cost what was then the astronomical price of 990

Belgian francs each. The form mentioned that a disagreement occurred between Cachet and the original clients because the statues portrayed naked ladies, but they were already cast and were eventually placed on the ship anyway.

From the pictures it was clear that many more bronze statues were to be found on the wreck. In other compartments, such as the first class music room, there was a description of five bronze panels that depicted five different Dutch heroes and scientists: Huygens, Michiel de Ruyter, Maarten Tromp, Prins Maurits and Hugo de Groot. The door panels were decorated with inlaid tin and depicted the planet Saturn. The smoking room was also finished with bronze panels, and had a marble bust of Huygens.

The *Christiaan Huygens* docked in a foreign port.

Passengers giving scale to the massive ship.

A servant next to one of the statues raised off the wreck.

Passengers relaxing on deck.

The ship even had a souvenir shop.

Above: The interior of the ship.

SEARCHING THE WRECK

It was very difficult to find precisely where the statues would be on the wreck, but after many dives and studies of the plans I could focus on an area that must have been the first class dining hall. A recurring problem was dropping the anchor as close as possible to the site of the statues; on a wreck of 170m, this was not an easy task. However, a lot of practice meant we became much better at interpreting the sonar images, thus solving the problem. For weeks the site was combed centimetre by centimetre, and finally on 27th July I was successful and found a bronze owl and a cat in between two beams. On the following three days I found three other statues in the same location. Several years later I found one of the bronze panels that had served as decoration of the support beams in the first class dining hall. Since then other divers also found statues in the wreck.

DIVING THE *HUYGENS*

In fifteen years I have logged more than 200 dives on the wreck. The visibility can vary from just a few centimetres to 8m, but usually it is not that good as the ship is positioned on a sandbank; this is also the main reason it is difficult to find your way around. During neap tide long dives can be made on the wreck; however, during springtide the water barely comes to a standstill, and there are very strong currents. The depth of the wreck is between 8 and 25m at the bow. She has been ripped apart by waves and current, but it is still possible to enter some areas with the use of a reel.

The spacious interior.

Details after preservation.

Stefan with a bronze statue.

Cannon   Crane.

Staircase with underwater photo of the mosaic floor.

The engines are still clearly recognisable and now form the tallest points on the wreck. There is a cannon at the stern, and at the bow there is another, beautiful, one on a pedestal. Close to this area is an ammunition room, which is still stocked with grenades. (The ship sailed as troop transport during the war.) The cranes that were placed at various locations on the ship to take on cargo have fallen beside the wreck and make a great orientation point to start your exploration. The wreck is located at 51.37.05 north/003.16.73 east. The *Huygens* still is one of my favourite wrecks to dive but it certainly has its quirks!

The wreck is also a great hideout for numerous crabs and lobsters that reside in the scrap. Large schools of sea bass call the wreck their home as well, but go into hiding as soon as divers arrive on the wreck.

When I made my first wreck dive of the year this season the visibility was barely 20cm. This made exploration a dangerous undertaking, and a certain amount of caution was necessary.

However, the MS *Christiaan Huygens* is a fantastic wreck to explore, and I am sure it will offer up many more of its secrets in the coming years.

Inserted picture left top: Engine builder's plate.
Inserted picture right top: The bell with a weight of 60kg
Other photographs: Items found on the wreck after preservation.

Ladder.

Bottles.

Anchor.

The bow.

SS *NATAL*

COLLISION IN THE NIGHT

On board the beautiful ocean liner the SS *Natal* on
the night of 30 August 1917 were several first-class
passengers who placed their valuable gold and
jewellery in the ship's safe. The vessel sank barely
ten minutes after a collision at night.

Foto:Drazen Goricki

SS Natal

Type: Passenger ship
Built: La Ciotat, France, 1881
Owner: Messageries Maritimes
Propulsion: Steam engine/sail
Tonnage: 4,400 tons
Dimensions: Length 130m, beam 12m

Souvenir de Voyage

« CALÉDONIEN »
Paquebot Français des Messageries Maritimes

Sistership of the Natal.
Previous page: The wreck still stands proud.

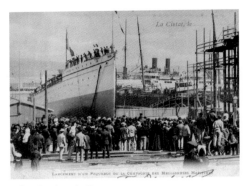

Photos of the wharf where the *Natal* was built.

The SS *Natal* was capable of carrying more than 1,300 passengers, but took on only 503 during its last fateful boarding in Marseille. Once aboard they were free to enjoy the luxury of this ship during their journey to Madagascar and rumours circulated that several rich people were on board who were fleeing the war with their fortunes. As it was wartime the captain ordered a complete blackout to hide the ship from the enemy.

The SS *Natal* was built in 1881 by Messageries Maritime in La Ciotat, France. She was a beautiful ship with luxurious decoration and passengers travelled in great comfort. When the order to sail was given the visibility was poor, but nothing that would cause undue concern. The captain watched from the bridge as the crew cast off and the vessel slid away from the docks. Slowly, the speed was increased until the three-cylinder compound steam engine reached its maximum pressure.

Several miles from port the visibility suddenly became worse and the captain ordered a reduction in speed, as it was dangerous and he wanted to avoid a collision. It was a very dark night with a heavily overcast sky, and the visibility reduced by the minute. The first class passengers were enjoying a glass of wine or a cup of coffee when the liner was hit at full speed by a French cargo ship.

SAVE OUR SOULS

It was as if the ship was forced to a stop by a giant hand. Tables and chairs were thrown about and passengers were flung to the deck. They started to run around in panic while the crew tried to obey the orders of the officers. As the ship was taking on

Menu of a dinner on the sistership.

Foto: Drazen Goricki

Diver scootering over the wreck.

water quickly, the lifeboats were turned out straight away, and the crew tried to get the passengers into them once the first panic had subsided. Meanwhile, the SS Natal had started to list, hampering the evacuation. On the lower decks, where the third-class passengers were accommodated, the water had already entered, causing many passengers to drown. The radio officer had been trying to send an SOS message, but it quickly became apparent that the ship would not stay afloat much longer and the captain gave the order to abandon ship. As the liner sank deeper and deeper, a number of people jumped overboard in panic trying to save themselves. Barely ten minutes after the collision the SS Natal sank with the captain still on board. Seventy-six passengers and twenty-eight crew members did not survive.

Expedition ship.

AN UNDERWATER MUSEUM AT 130M DOWN

The wreck of the SS Natal can be found 4 miles south of the island lighthouse Le Planier, at a depth of 130m. The sonar images made it clear that the vessel was standing upright on its keel. Due to its depth

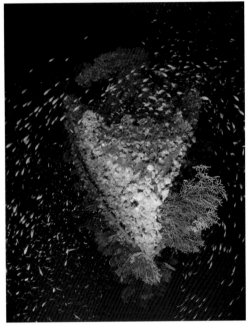
Bow of the wreck covered in fish (D. Goricki).

and distance from the shore the wreck is difficult to reach and proved to be a time capsule from 1881 – filled with artefacts. A sturdy boat is needed to sail the 12 miles, which is only possible when the conditions are ideal – not much wind and minimum wave height are a must.

Using normal air is impossible during such a dive; the solution is a gas mixture containing helium in combination with a rebreather. A rebreather can enlarge the bottom time by recycling and scrubbing the breathing gas in a closed circuit clean of dangerous carbon dioxide. An underwater scooter is needed to be able to explore the full length of the wreck. The next problem we faced was putting together a team that was able to make such extreme deep dives.

Divers on decompression.

Philippe Peyruss, captain of the expedition ship.

ORGANISATION OF A COMPLEX DIVE

To compile the team I called on Pim van der Horst, a highly experienced rebreather diver and chairman of DIRrebreather. The DIRrebreather group has undertaken many expeditions and consists of members of different countries in Europe. For this expedition the group consisted of: Pim van der Horst (Netherlands), Eveline Verdier (France), Alexandre Fox (France), Frank Gentile (France), Vic Verlinden (Belgium), Armando Ribeiro (Portugal), Marco Valenti (Italy), Christophe Brieger (Germany) and Drazen Goricki (Croatia).

The dive centre Passion in La Ciotat was used as our base during this expedition. The owner of the centre was Philippe Peyruss, who was also the captain of the boat we wanted to use.

It was early in the morning when the group came together in the port and began loading. Nine rebreathers and twenty-seven dive cylinders of 12 litres each were

Remains of the wooden deck (D. Goricki).

Divers on the line.

Starboard completely covered in marine growth.

Marco Valenti.

taken on board. On top of this came the extra equipment, including four scooters, making the boat fully loaded. The weather was favourable with almost no wind. However, this early in the morning it was already warm and we had to make sure we drank plenty of water so we did not become dehydrated during the dive.

After approximately ninety minutes' sailing we reached the wreck location. The placing of the down line was an intricate task and captain Philippe took his time sailing over the wreck several times before he dropped its heavy weight. When the line was placed, the dive teams and the sequence of dives were arranged. I would dive with Armando, Pim and Eveline in the third team. The agreement we made was that we would descend for five minutes and have ten minutes bottom time. It would then take about three hours for our safe return to the surface.

FIRST EXPLORATION OF THE WRECK

While preparing for the dive we got help when attaching the bailout bottles (our back-up in case of a rebreather problem), which was a great help as it had now become quite warm. After jumping in the water the group gathered at the buoy of the down line to conduct a last check before Pim gave the signal to descend. The visibility in the water was murky for the first 15m but clear further down. During the descent we took time to get used to the rebreathers and after about five minutes I could see the wreck below me. While on top of the deck I was at a depth of 122m, and not far off I could see one of the large masts lying on the deck. From what I could see I reckoned we were between the foremast and the bow. Meanwhile, Armando had started to film and we swam together along the deck, its wooden planking still discernible. The wreck was overgrown with anemones and coral, making it difficult to recognise parts of it. We had to be extremely cautious as we swam along the deck, as it was covered in numerous fishing nets and lines.

Swimming a little further on, I recognised one of the windows that had been used to light up the below decks. The ten minutes of bottom time were over before

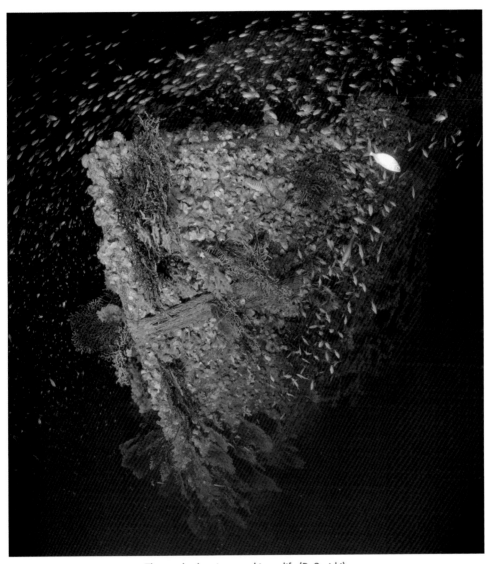

The wooden bow is covered in sealife (D. Goricki).

The dive team.

we knew it, and soon it was time to start our ascent. This took three long hours, and during the last part of it I started to feel the cold as the water was only 9 degrees at the last decompression stop at 6m. I was therefore happy to see the sun shining when we returned.

SECOND DEEP DIVE IN THREE DAYS

During our second deep dive we planned for the same ten-minute bottom time. The dive teams changed around a bit. I now dove in a team with Pim and Armando, and our goal was to get a better idea of the condition of the wreck. The weather was still fine with light winds when we reached the wreck site at around 10:00. Again, nothing was left to chance, and the dive gear, including rebreathers, were checked thoroughly. While waiting on each other in the water we noticed that the visibility was extremely poor. We could barely see 3m ahead and big flakes of sediment were floating around in the water.

Luckily, that changed the deeper we descended, and on the wreck the visibility was excellent. On top of the deck I noticed two large holes of about 4 sq m to the left of me. Here I looked inside the wreck and noticed we could descend a further 10m into the wreck, going deeper than we could outside it. Inside the wreck I could see parts of the engine room. Meanwhile, I noticed Drazen Goricki was still taking pictures of the vessel.

We stayed on top of the deck and swam to the other side, where I found a bronze cylinder that looked like a part of a telegraph. Here we noticed considerably fewer fishing nets and lines. According to my estimation we were now at the midship. Here we found a large branch of white coral that had grown on the side of the wreck. Next, we swam back to the side, where we placed the down line and followed the edge along the bow. Armando was still busily filming when we gave the signal to ascend. With a final glance backwards to this beautiful wreck, which still had much to discover, we started our long, slow ascent towards the surface. In future years the SS *Natal* will surely give up more of its secrets.

ROOMPOT

SUNK EIGHT MILES FROM HER HOME PORT

When the *Roompot* had almost reached her home port after a journey that had taken more than nine months, fate struck mercilessly. A heavy storm sent the ship to the bottom of the North Sea, where she lay untouched by man for more than 140 years.

Roompot

Type: Frigate
Built: De geode intentie, Zierikzee, Netherlands
Owner: De Crane, Zierikzee, Netherlands
Propulsion: sails
Tonnage: 719 tons
Dimensions: Length 42m, beam 9m
Cargo: rice

A soya bottle, ricebowl and a gingerpot
found on the wreck.
Previous page: One of the masts.

The crew liked to play a game now and then,
witnessed by the find of these pieces.

On 25th September 1852 the East India ship the *Roompot* sailed from her home port of Zierikzee in the Netherlands. The wooden frigate was departing on a six-month journey to the East Indian Archipelago (now Indonesia). The ship was a mere 719 tons and below the waterline she was covered in sheet copper to protect her against shipworms. The *Roompot* had been built ten years earlier at the shipyard de Goede Intentie (the good intention) for the shipping company The Crane of Zierikzee. Twenty-two crew members were hired for this trip under the command of Captain De Boer. The journey went smoothly and the ship docked on 4th February 1853 in Akiab, a harbour on the west coast of Burma. During the next few days the ship was loaded with a large cargo of rice. On 20th February, Captain De Boer gave the order to raise the anchor and the *Roompot* started the long and dangerous journey back to Zierikzee.

BEACHED

The *Roompot* got its share of bad weather during its return journey and the pumps often needed to be manned to keep the holds dry and maintain a reasonable speed. The ship arrived in poor condition at the entrance to Dartmouth, England, on 27th June. The next day the pilot cutter Flushing no. 2 came alongside to report that there were no qualified pilots available. However, it transferred two apprentice pilots, Cornelis Dekker and Marinus Engels, to the *Roompot*.

Shortly after noon on 29th June, the church tower of Westkapelle on the Dutch coast became visible. Some while later the ship unexpectedly hit a sandbar with a terrible jolt. The ship immediately started to take on water, and the captain ordered one sloop with eight crew members to be lowered. As the situation was deteriorating minute by minute, the captain decided to lower the second sloop and take his place on it. However, this boat was overturned by a large wave, drowning three crew members including the ship's doctor. The captain and the others managed to climb back on board and later succeeded in reaching the shore in a small work boat.

THE SINKING

From their vantage point on the 'Long John' (the nickname for the bell tower in the Abbey of Middelburg), the tower keepers, Wezepoel and Landman, noticed that the ship floated free again at high tide and drifted into the Roompot channel. Several fishermen saw the ship, with some even going aboard and anchoring her in front of the Veeregat channel, where she eventually sank. On

Vic and Frank, ready to go.

30th June the masts were still visible, but one day later they were gone, lost forever. After years sailing around the world, the *Roompot* sank in a channel of the same name just a few miles from her home port.

THE DISCOVERY

It was 15th August 1992 and we anchored on top of an underwater object several miles from West Kapelle. As often happened, we got this position from a fisherman, and at the time it was believed to be the wreck of the *Cristina* (a fishing vessel). We decided to take a closer look. Diving a new wreck is always an exciting adventure as you never know what you will find. As we mostly sailed with just the two of us on the boat, myself and Frank de Bode, our habit was to dive solo while the other stayed topside. During this dive Frank would mind the boat and I would make the first explorative dive. First we had to wait for the tide to slacken, as we found ourselves close to the Oosterschelde Dam and it would be too dangerous to drift.

During the descent along the down line, the current was still noticeable and visibility was less than a metre. At a depth of 20m I landed on the seabed, where I found some wooden beams. The diving conditions were so bad I decided not to

Articles in the newspapers after the discovery of the wreck.

Aquarelle of the *Roompot*.

Glassware, chinaware and bottles found on the wreck.

leave the down line. I looked around some more and discovered a black glass bottle in between the wooden beams.

After surfacing, I noticed it was a hand-blown bottle and decided to make a second dive on the wreck. The visibility was still as bad; however, I was lucky as the anchor had fallen on a good spot on the wreck. When I arrived on the bottom I found myself in between several wine bottles of different shapes, a brass horn and a porcelain ginger jar. In between all these artefacts I discovered a golden ring carrying the initials 'P.J.B'. All these clues made me think it was a virgin wreck

Divers with the raised bell.

Precious rings.

Brass speaking tube.

Mast on the forecastle of the wreck.
Inserted picture: Diver ready to splash.

Silver tableware.

– untouched since it sank. To discover the vessel's identity, however, it would be necessary to recover an object with the name of the shipping company.

After a sleepless night, tension was in the air before the first longer dive. While I descended I noticed the visibility had improved somewhat compared to the previous day. The anchor had hooked behind a wooden beam on the wreck, but otherwise there was nothing but sand. I attached my reel to the down line and swam. At about 10m from the down line I noticed a semi-circular shape in the sand. I immediately felt deeper with my hands and when I pulled the object clear, with some considerable difficulty, a beautiful ship's bell appeared in front of me with the name *Roompot* on it.

PROTECTED MONUMENT

Shortly after the discovery the wreck was registered at the Netherlands Institute for Ship and Underwater Archaeology (NISA) and is now a protected monument. Contact was also made with the city of Zierikzee to make a movie about the wreck, but negotiations were stopped due to a lack of funding.

Frank and I decided to make and finance a film about the wreck ourselves. Although not of the highest quality, the film has become a unique document of the wreck. On the film you can see that the cargo of rice is still present. The rice, in hessian sacks, had been covered by sand and sediment down the years and so it was preserved. Several artefacts were recovered that may in time find a place in the Maritime Museum in Zierikzee.

These objects were not only large but also small items such as lead balls intended for use in muskets. We also found an iron cannon on the aft of the ship the following year, a surprise as we always presumed she did not have any heavy armament. Years later the NISA started its own archaeological excavation and it found and conserved a checkerboard. NISA proved that the *Roompot* was an important wreck

The bow.

Part of the rudder.

On the way to the wreck site.

Grinding stone.

but it is unfortunate that, due to a lack of funds, a full excavation has not been carried out.

Diving on the wreck is permitted, but it is forbidden to take artefacts. The *Roompot* lies between 18 and 25m and is positioned north/south, bow/stern. The bow still rises about 5m from the sand and is the most recognisable part. One of the heavy masts that were broken during the storm can be found at the bow. The aft is still recognisable by the rudderpost, and even the cargo of rice is still largely present.

THE THEFT

Years after the discovery of the wreck, more and more information surfaced from the archives about the *Roompot*. A researcher named Schwartz discovered that Captain Hendrik de Boer of the *Roompot* had walked along the market square in Zierikzee three months after the wrecking of his ship and stopped at a stall, his curiosity piqued by some navigational instruments for sale. He was astonished to find his own binoculars, compass and sextant! He immediately reported the theft to the police. From the first court hearing it appeared that, after the first grounding, the pilot Bernardus Taberne had boarded the *Roompot* and stolen the instruments.

BALOERAN
THE FLOATING PALACE

Decorated with the finest materials, the motor ship *Baloeran* was the pride of the shipping company Rotterdam Lloyd. When it left the Fijenoord shipyard in March 1929 nobody could envision that it would suffer such an inglorious end.

Baloeran

Type: Passenger ship
Built: Fijenoord Yard, Rotterdam
Owner: Rotterdamse Lloyd
Propulsion: Double screw, diesel engine
Length: 175m, beam 21m
Speed: 21 knots

Aquarelle of the *Baloeran*.
Previous page: Diver descends onto the wreck

Cross-section blueprint of the ship.

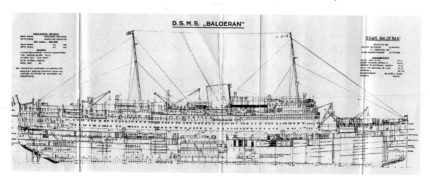

When the ship started its sea trials on 9th April 1930 it managed a speed of 20 knots. As it measured 16,000 BRT, this was a considerable achievement at the time. The MS *Baloeran* could transport 234 first-class passengers and 280 second-class passengers, and it had a crew of 317 that made sure the pampered passengers lacked nothing during their trip to Batavia (Jakarta).

The journeys on the *Baloeran* and her sister ship *Dempo* were legendary as they were equipped with the latest designs and decor. On board there was a swimming pool, a smoking room, a reading room and a kindergarten. Every day the passengers could enjoy large buffets or order from an á la carte menu in the first-class restaurant. During a voyage in the summer of 1932 the Belgian royal couple Leopold and Astrid were guests on the *Baloeran*. As a thank you they sent a picture with a handwritten message to the shipping company.

The *Baloeran* passing the Maas bridge.

On the wharf in Rotterdam.

Stern of the ship with the Nazi flag.

The luxury decoration and furniture.

Five years after the *Baloeran* was launched, she was modernised at the Smit shipyard in Rotterdam. This raised her total weight to more than 17,000 tons. However, the start of the Second World War had a major impact on the company and the amount of sailings had to be curbed as passenger numbers declined.

TAKEN OVER BY HOSTILE POWERS

In the Koninklijke Rotterdamse Lloyd museum one can still admire some of the original furniture.

On 31st August 1939 the *Baloeran* entered the port of Dandong in the Dutch East Indies after a journey from Rotterdam. After the necessary maintenance and refuelling, the homeward journey began on 13th September. The ship was supposed to depart again from Rotterdam for Batavia on 11th December. However, this was cancelled due to the threat of hostilities, and the *Baloeran* remained in Rotterdam.

The Nazis invaded the Netherlands the following May and when they needed a suitable hospital ship they requisitioned the *Baloeran* and had it modified at the Wilton-Fijenoord Shipyard. The vessel, renamed the *Strasbourg*, was now able to carry 500 sick military personnel and 161 medical staff. However, the German crew thought it rolled too much and was too difficult to steer, so it was brought back to the shipyard. After much

The *Baloeran*, sunk on a bank after the attack.

The attack on the ship seen from one of the aircraft.

Baloeran in war colors.

investigation and some modifications, *Strasbourg* ship made a few trips between Germany and Norway. On 31st August 1943 she left port bound for Hamburg.

When the *Strasbourg* was passing along the coast off Ijmuiden, Netherlands, an intense explosion occurred close to the engine room: the ship had run into a floating mine. In the following days attempts were made to save the ship, but it began to sink and several attacks by British planes and the firing of a torpedo by a fast boat put paid to these hopes. The once beautiful liner was now a wreck, lost forever just miles from the

Hugo Geijteman, a passionate wreck diver.

shore. Her sister ship the *Dempo* served as troop transport ship, but she was torpedoed and sank in the Mediterranean in 1944.

A LOVED DIVING OBJECT

Over the years many salvage projects have taken place on the wreck as it contained lots of copper and many other precious metals. Sport divers have also explored the vessel, which has a length of almost 190m. The ship has broken into pieces, making the debris field even larger. The seabed in this area is between 6 and 10m at low tide, and the visibility is poor, especially in the spring.

The best months to dive on the wreck are July and August, especially on a slack tide. The original bronze letters with the name have been taken off the wreck by sport divers and gifted to the maritime museum Prins Hendrik in Rotterdam. Numerous other artefacts have been recovered by sport divers and have found a place as souvenirs to a ship with a colourful past.

HUGO GEIJTEMAN: WRECK DIVER IN HEART AND SOUL

One of the first sport divers to dive on the *Baloeran* regularly was Hugo Geijteman. His story shows how wreck diving on the North Sea by motivated sport divers became popular. Hugo made his first North Sea dive as a member of the sports diving club Haarlem. In those early days there was not enough money to buy a proper boat and everyone had to help out.

Hugo cobbled together a diving platform out of two drop tanks from a Starfighter jet with the help of some friends and thus made it to the wreck site. As the wreck was marked by buoys, no navigation equipment was necessary and the group could find the wreck with the anchor. In this way they could make some nice dives and salvage some copper to cover the costs. Several years later they could afford a rigid inflatable boat with GPS navigation equipment, enabling them to reach wrecks that were not buoyed. In 1997 Hugo became a regular crew member on the ship *Zeester of Klaas Koch*, on which he visited many previously uncharted wrecks.

SS *EGYPT*

THE GOLD OF THE SS *EGYPT*

The recovery of gold and silver from the wreck of the SS *Egypt* counts as one of the biggest successes in the field of salvage. The wreck lies at a depth of 130m, deeper than any salvage company had ever worked before.

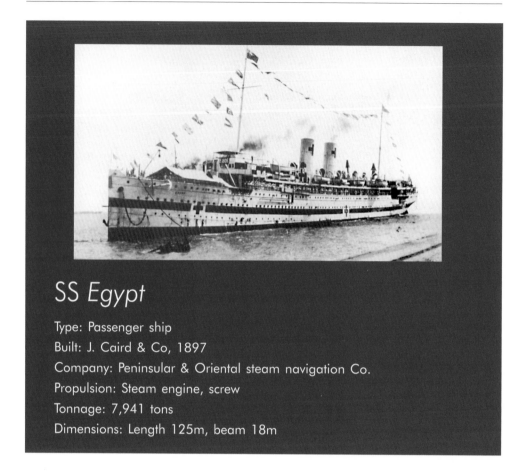

SS *Egypt*

Type: Passenger ship
Built: J. Caird & Co, 1897
Company: Peninsular & Oriental steam navigation Co.
Propulsion: Steam engine, screw
Tonnage: 7,941 tons
Dimensions: Length 125m, beam 18m

In 1897 the keel was laid for a new ship for the Peninsular & Oriental Steam Navigation Co. at the shipyard of J. Caird & Co. in Glasgow, Scotland. The passenger ship SS *Egypt*, employed on the Indian line of P&O, was 165m long and had a gross tonnage of almost 8,000 tons. Over the course of more than twenty years the ship sailed without incident and became one of P&O's oldest ships. On 19th May 1922, the SS *Egypt* left London, where forty-four passengers and 294 crew members had embarked along with a cargo of 10 tons of gold and 5 tons of silver with a value at that time of more than £1 million. She set sail for Marseille, where she would pick up more passengers before she would continue on towards Bombay. The next day, as the ship neared the island of Ushant, of Brittany, a thick fog hung over the Channel and the captain gave the order for slow steaming and then to stop all engines. Through the thick fog the crew now heard the fog horn of another ship but they could not see her or discern where she was. The other ship was the SS *Seine*, under the command of Captain Le Barzic, which was on its way from La Pallice to Le Havre. Captain Le Barzic had departed from the usual coastal route to be further out at sea to avoid Ushant.

On the bridge of the *Egypt* it was presumed that all the other ships in the area would be on parallel courses. When another ship suddenly broke through the fog

Previous page: winch on the bow

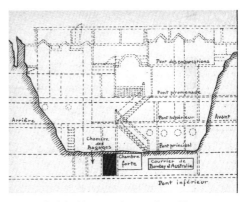

Gold bars being stacked.

Detail of the blueprint showing the golden room.

it was too late for any evasive action and the SS *Seine* crashed into the starboard side of the *Egypt*'s hull. The blow was of such force that a large crack appeared and the ship started to sink.

PANIC ON BOARD

The crew members started to lower the boats in panic, however, the calm and order needed to organise a safe disembarkation was missing. They were also hampered in their actions as the ship began to list heavily. When the SS *Egypt* started to sink further, all lines holding the life rafts and lifeboats were cut so they could float free when it finally went down. This action saved many lives. The SS *Seine* had slowly drifted away from the SS *Egypt* into the fog but returned to pick up any survivors, who were brought on board by Captain Le Barzic and his crew. After a head count it was discovered that sixty-five people were missing and four were dead. Twenty-nine passengers and 210 crew members of the P&O liner survived the disaster. Several heroic actions took place, such as the officer who ordered the crew of his lifeboat to return to the scene, thus saving seventy people. The captain remained on board and was taken off by one of the lifeboats. The radio officer of the SS *Egypt* also remained on board until the last moment to send the ship's location to other vessels. The radio stations on the shore could also pick up these signals and as such could make a cross-reference of the position

LE PRIME NOTIZIE DEL NAUFRAGIO PUBBLICATE NEL GIORNALE DEL *LLOYD'S* IL MATTINO DI LUNEDÌ 22 MAGGIO 1922.

The disaster was discussed in detail In Lloyd's journal.

The Italian newspaper *La Domenica del Corriere*, June 1930.

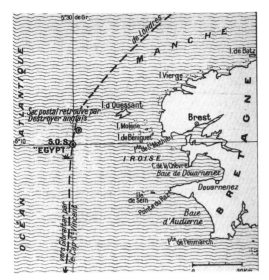

The location of the wreck.

of the sinking ship. The radio officer paid with his life for his heroic actions, going down with the ship. After the disaster there was much discussion about who was responsible for the collision, but no conclusion was ever reached.

SEARCHING FOR A NEEDLE IN A HAYSTACK

Starting in the year the SS *Egypt* sank many French and Swedish salvage companies tried to find the wreck and retrieve the gold. This was no easy task, as the ship was lying roughly 30 miles offshore and the salvors lacked the locating equipment we have today. The only information available was a rough position and cross-reference provided by the shore-based radio stations. One after another the salvage companies gave up, until in June 1929 the Italian Maritime Salvage Association (Sorima) under Commandatore Giovanni Quaglia decided to try its luck.

The company had gained experience in deep diving on another wreck in the vicinity. The Belgian ship *Elisabethville* of the Compagnie Maritime Belge sank close to the island Belle île with a cargo of ivory and diamonds and rested at a depth of 80m. Sorima succeeded in finding the wreck and removing the safe. Unfortunately, the diamonds were not there, but it was able to recover the precious ivory. During this operation the company gained a lot of experience with the Neufeldt and Kuhnke diving suit, which had moveable arms and legs. But first the wreck of the SS *Egypt* needed to be found, and this was to take much longer than expected.

The main method used in the search consisted of towing a steel wire suspended between two ships at a certain depth above the seabed. The ships were about 900m apart and the wire was almost 1,500m long. According to the maps, the bottom was supposed to be flat in this area, which in fact turned out to be wrong. Every time the wire made contact with something a diver was sent down to check if it was the wreck. This was a time-consuming method as the wire often caught on a rock or the wrong wreck. To be able to lower the Neufeldt and Kuhnke on the right spot it was necessary to anchor the ship before lowering it. A simpler one-atmosphere diving suit was also made, which was easier to maintain and use, and enabled work to proceed at a quicker pace. Once contact with the bottom was made, the diving cylinder was lowered with the first diver, Gianni. However, the current was so strong it pulled the cylinder on its side and kept it at a depth of about 20m. When the steel towing wire also broke it was pulled back aboard covered in white paint, indicating it had snagged on something. The team thought it could not be the SS *Egypt*, as she had a black hull and black chimneys, but Quaglia recalled that the ship had served as a hospital ship in the First World War and had been painted

Father Innocentius failed to find the wreck with his divining rods.

The model allowed the divers to plan how to salvage the gold.

white. Unfortunately the weather then turned bad, so a buoy was laid and course was set towards the port of Brest to wait for better conditions. When the Sorima team returned several days, later the buoy had disappeared and the exact location could not be found any more. Another fifteen months would pass before the ship was finally found again at almost the exact spot the crew had lost the buoy. With just a little luck the salvors would have found the wreck fifteen months earlier.

THE DIVINING ROD OF FATHER INNOCENTIUS

While the Sorima team was still searching to find the ship for the second time, Commandatore Quaglia wanted to call on the Capuchin monk Father Innocentius, who reportedly possessed the gift of being able to find a steel mass or gold from the water's surface. The other crew members did not believe in this ability, however, Quaglia persisted and had Father Innocentius join the search. He used a twig with three ends, of which he held two as a divining rod to determine the location of the wreck. However, when his method was tried at sea it soon became apparent that the father could not deliver on his promise and valuable time was lost. The monk was quickly sent on his way back to Paris.

Several other charlatans tried to convince Quaglia of their special gifts, but from that point on only his crew were trusted in the search. The bad weather hampered the work, meaning the salvors could only work for about ten days each month. The downtime was spent in the port of Brest or trying their luck on other wrecks. Finally, on 30th June 1930, they returned to the SS *Egypt* with some unexpected help in the form of Captain Le Barzic of the SS *Seine*, who joined the salvage ship *Artiglio*. On the day of the collision he spent three hours on the scene, and had made notes about the position. After several days luck was on their side; when they tried to recover one of the buoys that had drifted, a piece of iron was stuck to its line. This piece had the same dimensions as the davits of the SS *Egypt*. At last, they were closing in on the wreck and its treasure.

3 photos: The *Artiglio's* crew.

Crew holding the gold bars.

The safe is hauled aboard.

The claw spits some more gold!

WHERE IS THE GOLD?

Early the next morning the crew of the *Artiglio* positioned several buoys to enable them to place the ship precisely above the wreck. Diver Francechi took his place in the observation cylinder, which was closed by Gianni. The cylinder went over the side and the descent to the wreck started. Everyone waited anxiously for Francechi's messages. It took a while before his eyes were accustomed to the ambient light on the wreck but he soon started to recognise parts, and the sight of the giant steam windlasses on the deck removed all doubt. On the deck of the *Artiglio* the crew cheered with joy as the SS *Egypt* and its five tons of gold was found.

Now the real work on the wreck could start. The divers had a cardboard model of the ship so they could get a better idea of where the gold should be. Quickly, they discovered that the stern was damaged but the bow was still intact. The *Artiglio* was now moored on four anchors, which could be slacked or tensioned to position the ship in the spot the divers wanted. Gianni had discovered places on the deck where they could place explosives to open up the underlying decks, where the gold had been stowed. After barely forty-eight hours of work the crew succeeded in bringing one of the six-ton cargo booms to the surface. When they entered the port

Diver illuminates one of the ship's bollards.

Anchor lying on the foredeck.

of Brest with the boom it became clear to even the loudest of their critics that they would be able to reach the gold and salvage it. As it was late in the season, Quaglia decided to remove the *Artiglio* from the *Egypt* and work on some of the wrecks in the bay of Quiberon. Unfortunately, the *Artiglio* itself became a wreck when she was working on a vessel packed with explosives; a misjudgement caused the entire wreck to explode and sink the ship above.

ANOTHER SHIP IS BOUGHT

During the winter another ship was sought to replace the *Artiglio*. Eventually, an old fishing ship was found and converted into a salvage ship using the old cargo booms recovered from the SS *Egypt*. The *Artiglio II* was ready to return to the wreck site in July. The crew consisted of sailors from other ships owned by Sorima under command of Captain Carli. The divers Gianni, Franceschi and Bargellini came back on board to resume their task. In early August the upper deck of the presumed location of the gold was removed. The treasure chamber was deep inside, and they first had to fight their way through six decks to reach it, taking time, patience and lots of skill from the divers. The darkness and the current at a depth of 130m were also big hindrances that would have to be overcome. The divers often had to wait for the current to subside before they could place the explosive charges in the right spot. As the current ran continuously it was a time consuming job. The steel diving suit also could not be employed as often as first thought; the current merely used the suit as a plaything, and so it could not always be placed in the desired positions. Still, the divers worked themselves deeper and deeper using the crane grab to pull pieces from the wreck. Despite working until December 1931, they did not succeed in reaching the gold that year. When the team were back in position above the wreck in June 1932 they only had to remove some remaining parts of the main deck to reach the treasure chamber. Meanwhile, they had

Intensive testing of the equipment before this challenging dive.

About to jump.

created a big pile of steel from all the pieces they had removed. When they had removed the last deck the big grab was replaced by a smaller one so it could work inside the treasure chamber. First, only junk and pieces of wood were brought to the surface (some of the wood could have been from boxes in which the gold had been). Then the grab surfaced full of Indian rupee bank notes that had also been in the cargo.

Finally at the Gold

When more rupees came to the surface they were stored in baskets as there was no place to dry them out. On 22nd June, after a period of bad weather, the salvage crew was back in position and the grab was again pulling up junk and pieces of wood. However, someone then let out a yell and showed off a gold coin in his hands. A second coin was found, and they knew now they were on the right track.

Bollards and railing on the wreck.

Diver giving scale to a spare propeller blade.

In the afternoon the work continued and all waited anxiously until the grab surfaced again. At first sight it was the usual junk and mud, then with a dull thud two shining bars of gold fell on the deck.

More than four years after their quest for the gold began, they had finally reached it, and everyone on board started to congratulate each other. After the excitement had died down Commandatore Quaglia stood among his crew and spoke to them. He first asked for a moment of silence to remember some colleagues who had died in an explosion during a previous operation. Then he said this latest dive had accomplished something nobody had done before and would always have a place in history.

DIVING EXPEDITIONS TO THE WRECK

The wreck of the SS *Egypt* can be found at a depth of 125m and in years past it was unreachable for sport divers. However, due to the introduction of technical diving with rebreathers, wrecks such as this have become more accessible. In 2009 a group of seven English divers decided to organise an expedition to the wreck. After almost a year of planning and organisation, they boarded the expedition ship *Loyal Watcher* with Captain Darren at the wheel. The ship owners, Darren and Linda, were very experienced at organising diving expeditions, a necessity for a trip such as this. The ship was a former British Royal Navy tender and was built to withstand rough seas.

TESTING THE EQUIPMENT

On a dive like this the diving equipment is tested to its fullest. After a test dive on the wreck of the *Flying Enterprise* at a depth of 85m the team members were ready and the ship continued towards Ushant. The next day the anchor line with two buoys was dropped on the wreck. A final briefing was held in which the procedures for the dive were discussed, and the decision was made that they would always dive in buddy teams. Barry Smith and Neil Plant were the first buddy team and they had to fix the down line to the wreck. After a descent of five minutes they found themselves at a depth of 115m on the forward part of the ship close to the portside bollards. The visibility was more than 10m here. Their goal was to photograph as many different parts of the wreck as possible, which considering the short bottom time of twenty minutes was no easy task. During their short stay

Storage room.

Expedition team: Barry Smith (photographer), Neil Plant, Steve Brown, Bill Reed, Gabriele Paparo, Roy Smith and Toby Herbut.

they succeeded in taking pictures of the bow anchors and the spare propeller blade, which was still standing upright on the deck.

THE DECOMPRESSION OF HALF A WORKING DAY

The bottom time passed quickly, and the four-hour ascent was started. During this time the pairs were assisted by a safety diver, who could help them if something went wrong. The decompression station was disconnected from the down line at a depth of 60m so the divers would drift with the current while completing their stops. All dives went without problems, and during the last one Barry Smith and Steve Brown entered deep into the wreck. Here they discovered porcelain with the P&O logo and the lamp store of the ship. There was no trace of the gold that had not been recovered (2 per cent of the 5 tons) during the operations in 1930 and onwards. Still, the expedition was a success, with a total of 325 minutes of bottom time at an average depth of 115m. None of the divers experienced physical or technical problems apart from an issue with one of the scooters used that flooded due to a bad O-ring.

SS *KURSK*

THE CRYSTAL OF THE TSAR

Some North Sea shipwrecks hide valuable cargo that is discovered many years after the ship has been lost. For example, the SS *Kursk* contained a precious shipment of French Baccarat crystal. Worth a fortune in 1912, it was a luxury product only the richest could afford.

SS *Kursk*

Type: Steel cargo steamer
Built: Burmeister & Wain, Copenhagen, 1881
Company: DFDS
Propulsion: Steam engine/screw
Tonnage: 1,131 tons
Length: 80m, beam 14m
Speed: 8.5 knots

Tzar Nicolas ordered part of the *Kursk's* cargo.
Previous page: Diver with ceramic bottle

STORM ON THE NORTH SEA

During the night of 26th August 1912, a heavy storm, tracking south-west, was raging in the North Sea, putting a lot of ships in distress. One of these was the SS *Kursk*, on its way to St Petersburg, Russia. When berthed in Antwerp, an 8m granite column with a bronze eagle was placed in the hold of the 80m long ship – intended to be erected at Borodino, Russia, to commemorate the battle fought there against Napoleon in 1812. The French sculptor Paul Besanval designed the monument and would be personally supervising its placement in Russia. When the loading of the *Kursk* was completed, Captain Wiencke and the Belgian pilot wanted to leave quickly as the weather was becoming worse by the hour.

Vrijdag 16 november 2001

Limburger duikt zonder het te weten kristalschat boven

Berging van wrak van Kursk tijdelijk stopgezet

ANTWERPEN, VLISSINGEN - Er is herrie rond de Zeeuwse Kursk, het scheepswrak uit 1912 dat zopas door de Nederlandse onderwaterdetective Paul de Keijzer werd ontdekt ter hoogte van Goeree. Bootjes van de kustwacht controleren of sportduikers het bergingsverbod wel respecteren. De Nederlanders beschuldigen een Limburgse duiker ervan om al 1.300 stuks kristallen glaswerk

Reportage

mburger duikt kristalschat

anders beschuldigen Belg van 'plundering' scheepswrak Kursk

Kristin MATTHYSSEN

Kursk-ontdekker Paul de Keijzer (links) en zijn compagnon Cor Wauben tonen het kristal uit het wrak. Foto inzet: Het Diepree stortemerchip Kursk in 1912.

en Cor Wauben, Nederlandse onderwaterdetectives die het wrak van de Kursk 'officieel' ontdekten, met kristal van it.
(Foto René Oudshoorn)

Newspaper articles on the find of the crystal.

THE *KURSK* IS MISSING

The ship was built in 1881 at the Copenhagen shipyard of Burmeister & Wain, and was fitted with a 150hp steam engine. This was fired up by the stoker on the afternoon of 26th August 1912, and the SS *Kursk* commenced its long journey to Russia. When the ship was steaming down the Scheldt river the weather deteriorated, and once at sea a full-blown south-westerly storm developed, placing the *Kursk* in serious peril.

What happened next is anyone's guess. One of the theories is that the ship took a north-westerly course, and taking the waves broadside made the ship roll heavily. This rolling could have made the monument slide to one side, creating a sudden list and subsequent flooding. What is known is that none of the passengers or twenty-seven crew were able to launch the lifeboats in an attempt to save themselves. The next day several bodies washed ashore on the Zeeland coast, including Captain Wiencke's wife and the Belgian pilot. Some days later the newspaper noted that skipper H. Tanis of the fishing boat OD20 out of Ouddorp found a damaged white lifeboat carrying the name Kursk Kopenhaven offshore of Brouwershaven, close to Renesse, in the Netherlands.

A beautiful crystal decanter.

UNKNOWN WRECK AT 13 MILES

The wreck has been visited by divers for many years, although it was not until 1999 that a couple from Limburg found the first crystal in 1999 on the then unidentified ship. They kept their discovery a secret until a Dutch team led by Cor Wouben, who had nonetheless heard about the find, visited the wreck. This team found a small milk jug marked with the logo of the shipping company DFDS, the abbreviation of Det Forenede Dampskibsselskapet, Copenhagen. DFDS is still active and has a branch office in Belgium. When the story about the monument became known, the Netherlands Association for Ship and Underwater Archaeology (NISA) issued a salvage ban to protect the monument from treasure hunters.

DIVING THE *KURSK*

The salvage prohibition is still in force today and is enforced by the Dutch coastguard. The wreck is in the geographical position of 51.53.70 north/003.32.09 east. It is also marked on sea maps and is outside the shipping lanes. The top of the wreck is at a depth of 26m; however, if you drop down below the deck of the ship, a depth of 32m can be reached. The visibility can vary from centimetres, requiring divers to use a reel to navigate, to 6m on a good day.

The forward part of the wreck, up to the engine room, is buried under sand and silt. The engine room is still recognisable, but you need to watch out for fishing nets and lines in this area. The rear cargo hold contained the load of crystal, which has mostly been recovered. Another part of the cargo consisting of barrels is still visible, and over the edge at the stern you will find the propeller sticking up from the sand.

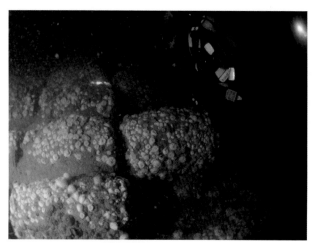

Barrels covered in growth.   Milk jug with the shipping line's crest.

Crystal found on the wreck.

Vic with his camera.

SS *LEERDAM*

EMIGRANTS AND PEDIGREE CATTLE

The crew of the SS *Leerdam* was taking on provisions and filling bunkers with coal as a heavy fog started to roll in. Captain Bruinsma wanted to leave as soon as possible, and when the fog lifted a little he gave the order to sail.

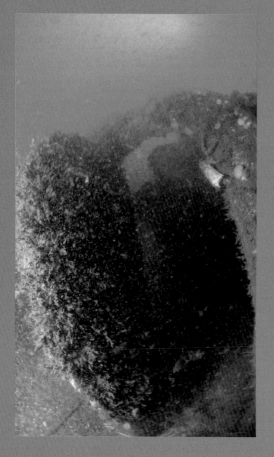

SS Leerdam

Type: Passenger ship
Build: Netherland shipbuilding company, 1881
Owner: NASM (Nederlands Amerikaanse Stoomvaart Maatschappij)
Propulsion: Steam/sail
Tonnage: 2,800 tons
Dimensions: Length 93m, beam 11m

Previous page left: Propeller. *Right*: Mast.

Shipping document.

Some 500 passengers were on board on 15th December 1889 for the voyage from the Netherlands to Argentina. Among them were many emigrants who were going to try their luck at the ship's final destination. The crew consisted of eighty-five men, five of them officers, and the captain. Besides the passengers, a large cargo of railway track and a number of pedigree cattle were on board. Twenty thoroughbred horses completed the list, making the ship fully loaded.

It was when the SS *Leerdam* was making its way through the fog, still in the vicinity of Dover that tragedy struck. The captain was by this time tired from being on the bridge for more than twenty-four hours without rest. Again and again he gave the order to slow down as it was too dangerous to make speed in the fog. He then

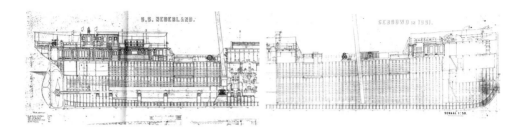

Cross-section blueprint of the ship.

ordered dead slow when someone heard the foghorn of another ship. Suddenly, the other ship appeared through the mist; it was too late for the SS *Leerdam* to avoid it, and she crashed into its hull.

One of the passengers later wrote in her report: 'It was foggy weather and very dark, still we steamed onwards. The first night on the SS *Leerdam* was quite tumultuous. I don't quite remember when all went to sleep, but I was not sleeping long before I was awakened as by a shot of a cannon. The whole ship was shaking, everything fell down. Even people fell from their bunks where they were sleeping. Firstly all were dismayed and were looking questioningly to each other. Then there was panic, most were walking around in nightgowns, whole families were holding hands thinking they were to perish. I was still too young to realise it all.'

RESCUE MISSION AT SEA

Captain Bruinsma gave his first officer the order to lower the lifeboats and organise the evacuation of the ship. He also had an emergency message sent by radio that was received by the cargo ship SS *Emma*, which immediately came to her aid. The *Emma* was a relatively small ship, however, her commander, Captain Basroger, was determined to save the *Leerdam*'s passengers. The vessel was heavily damaged and holed below the waterline, her engine room slowly filling with water.

When the *Emma* slowly closed on the sinking ship, Basroger spotted eight large and small lifeboats crammed with survivors. He called on them to come on board one by one so as to avoid more accidents. They were quickly served hot drinks and given blankets. The *Emma*'s crew did all they could to receive and help those onboard, and at the end of the rescue the ship was packed with more than 400 souls.

The other ship in the collision was the *Gaw Quan Sia*, a cargo vessel carrying a valuable load of tin. Those on board were not convinced she would remain afloat and the captain gave the order to lower the lifeboats. The crew tried to save the ship and let its pumps do their job, however, after some hours they had to abandon hope, and the *Gaw Quan Sia* took its cargo to the bottom. So it was on the SS *Leerdam*: pump or sink. The skeleton crew that remained on the ship tried all they could to patch the hole in the hull, but in the end they too had to give up. Eventually, the SS *Leerdam* also sank.

An illustration of the *Leerdam* in a gale at sea.

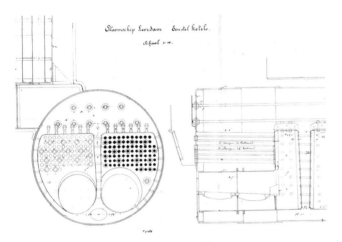

Plans of the ship's boilers.

.De Leerdam.

Omtrent de aanvaring van de *Leerdam* en de *Gaw Quan Sia* worden door de Ned. Amer. Stoomvaartmij nog de volgende bijzonderheden medegedeeld: De aanvaring had Maandag-ochtend te 2 uur, bij mistig weder, dertig mijlen benoorden Noord Hinder plaats. De kapitein van de *Leerdam* was tijdens de aanvaring zelf op de brug en alle voorzorgs-maatregelen waren stipt genomen. De aanva-ring was zoo hevig, dat de schepen in elkander liepen en niet konden worden gescheiden.

Des morgens te Dаur waren passagiers en bemanning overgegaan in de scheepssloopen, die in de nabijheid van de *Leerdam*, bleven totdat dit stoomschip des namiddags te 2 uur zonk. De opvarenden werden daarna door het Fransche stoomschip *Emma* opgenomen en werden Woensdagnamiddag te Cuxhaven aan land gebracht. Van daar zijn zij onder geleide van den kapitein en de officieren naar Hamburg vertrokken, alwaar intusschen alles tot hun ontvangst gereed was gemaakt.

Van particuliere zijde is een bericht ont-vangen, dat de gezagvoerder op voorbeeldige wijze de orde tijdens de ontscheping der schipbreukelingen heeft gehandhaafd, dewijl anders dit in volle zee, met ongeveer 450 passagiers aan boord, wel niet zonder onge-lukken zou zijn afgeloopen.

Het casco van het stoomschip *Leerdam* was ter Rotterdamsche Beurs verzekerd voor ƒ 300,000, waarvan ƒ 50,000 eigen risico door de N. A. S. M. wordt geloopen. Aan vracht-penningen is overigens ƒ 60,000 verzekerd. De lading is voor het grootste gedeelte aan de Beurs te Amsterdam gedekt.

Een van de geemployeerden der maatschappij is onmiddelijk naar Ostende vertrokken om de daar aangebrachte booten te onderzoeken.

De *Leerdam* had o. a. aan boord eenig Noord-Hollandsch stamboekvee en eenige paarden bestemd voor Buenos-Ayres, fraaie exemplaren, die natuurlijk den dood in de golven hebben gevonden. Tot de lading behoorden ongeveer 800 spoorwegrails en ongeveer 1000 ton stukgoed.

Articles describing the disaster.

FINALLY BACK ON SOLID GROUND

The *Emma* took the survivors to Hamburg, although even when they were safe on the ship there was a storm raging outside, and some of the lifeboats were smashed. Those on board feared that maybe this ship would also not survive. Their dream of a new life in another part of the world had suddenly turned into a nightmare. They were therefore relieved to be back on solid ground.

In Hamburg they could catch their breath, and they received aid from many charity organisations. Some of the passengers were determined to make the journey

A model of the ship.

Publicity posters of the
shipping line.

to Argentina and looked for a new ship. There was one group of fifty people from
the Dutch community Ferwerderadeel who, despite the setback, wanted to complete
the journey as they did not see any future for themselves in their own country.

SALVAGE OF A VALUABLE CARGO

When I joined a diving expedition in the English Channel in 2009, I came in contact
with Ian Taylor. He was the captain of the diving charter *Skin Deep*, which we were
travelling on. He told me of his work as a salvage diver in the 1990s, retrieving
the tin from the wreck of the *Gaw Quan Sia*. He used to be a salvage diver with

an English company and had gained information about the location and cargo of the wreck from a Belgian diving team. For several weeks they worked day and night to raise the tin treasure to the surface. The divers took turns and with each tide they penetrated deeper into the wreck's cargo hold. In this way they brought to the surface hundreds of tons of the valuable metal, which was sold for profit.

DIVING THE WRECK

The wreck of the SS *Leerdam* is located 35 miles off the Dutch coast, in the southern part of the North Sea. A good weather forecast with light winds is necessary to

A tile.

Part of a cup showing the shipping line's crest.

Collection of bottles.

Canned vegetables.

Selection of glass and stoneware salvaged from the wreck.

sail to a site this far out to sea. The wreck lies at a depth of 30m, with a maximum of 40m, and is heavily silted. Due to the currents and seawater, the wreck has completely fallen apart and turned into a debris field. Still, it is a nice dive because of the ship's history. Between 1880 and 1920 many emigrants tried to build a new future in the far away land of America, and the shipping industry played an important role in these journeys. You can still find reminders of emigrants on the wreck, as they usually travelled with all their possessions.

We also found a spare propeller blade on the wreck, which was carried to make repairs when one broke. Not much is left of the superstructure, but the rudder is still clearly visible. During one of my dives I found a piece of porcelain with the Nederlands Amerikaanse Stoomvaart Maatschappij (Netherland American steamship company, or NASM) logo on it. This was solid proof we were diving on the SS *Leerdam*. On the wreck we also found several glass preserving jars, which still contained vegetables. These were a curiosity as the contents were still recognisable after all these years. Wine bottles came in all shapes and sizes, and were found in different locations throughout the wreck.

Tiles with floral patterns (whiplash style) from the art nouveau period (1880–1900) could be seen on the wreck; these coincide with the building period of the SS *Leerdam* (1881). Ships in this period were decorated with the finest materials, especially in the first-class areas. The saloon and dining room for these passengers were decorated with teak furniture and brass chandeliers. All the tableware was made of silver, and the wine glasses and decanters were made of crystal. Compare that to the third-class areas, which were designed with the just the basics. Much of the silverware is now covered by the deck plates and hull of the wreck. No trace was found of the navigation bridge, with its telegraphs and bronze steering gear. Still, the *Leerdam* is a unique wreck with a beautiful story that has not yet come to an end.

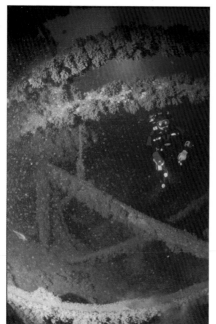

Bollards on the wreck.

Diver in one of the holds amidships.

SS WARRIOR

THE LOST BATTLE OF THE HMS *WARRIOR*

During both the First and Second World Wars many private
vessels were commandeered by the British Royal Navy.
These luxury yachts were often employed in dangerous
missions that did not always end well.

SS Warrior

Type: Luxury steam engine yacht
Built: UK
Propulsion: steam, twin screws
Tonnage: 1,100 tons
Dimensions: Length 100m, beam 12m

The *Warrior* was originally built as a luxury yacht for a private owner and was almost 100m long, extraordinary for this type of vessel. It was also equipped with two engines and was finished with expensive materials. The *Warrior* was originally named the *Goizeko Izarra*, and during her first years she fulfilled her duty as luxury transport. However, during the First World War she was commandeered to serve as a Navy vessel.

However, it was during the Second World War that this beautiful ship came to an end. On 11th July 1940 the *Warrior* was in the English Channel, roughly 20 miles from Weymouth, when it was attacked by a German plane. The pilot circled the ship once before deciding to attack. The *Warrior* took a direct hit and sank almost immediately, with one crew member losing his life.

DISCOVERY

A few years ago the wreck was found by the skipper of the Weymouth dive charter *Skin Deep*. One of the divers recovered the ship's bell, leading to the positive identification of the ship. When I visited the wreck myself, I sailed in *Skin Deep*

Previous page: Diver at the tiles by the swimming pool.

Diver Emanuel Feige.

Diver lift.

Captain Lennard, a very
experienced skipper.

The film crew.

Surfaced.

with a French group that had taken me in for a week. As the visibility in another part of the English Channel was bad we decided to visit wrecks further north. It is at times like this that it is crucial to have an experienced skipper to save your expensive diving week. According to our captain, Lennard, the visibility would be better around the *Warrior* because the seafloor there consists of gravel and pebbles, hence the current does not pick up any sand.

Lennard calmly kept his ship under control in every situation and was supported by his wife Maggy, who took care of the elevator that picked up the divers from the water. There were twelve technical divers on board, so the trip required a certain discipline to ensure all went smoothly. After the down line was placed, the first teams prepared to enter the water. There were several open circuit divers, and they entered first to ensure they would make their ascent roughly in time with the rebreather divers. It was all agreed the maximum dive time would not exceed two hours.

The huge boiler.

Engines.

PLAN YOUR DIVE AND DIVE YOUR PLAN

My buddy for the dive was a cave diver with a different type of rebreather to my own, therefore, we needed make some arrangements in case of an emergency. Dive planning is one of the most important things to discuss before you enter the water to explore a wreck at greater depths. The *Warrior* was at a depth of 54m, and we decided not to exceed the thirty-five-minute bottom time. After about ten minutes it was our turn to jump and slowly drift towards the buoy, but as several teams were to come after us we had to descend as quickly as possible. At 6m we took time to do a thorough bubble check to make sure the rebreather breathing loop was fully closed. At 45m we started to see parts of the wreck. The anchor of the down line was close to one of the steam boilers, and around this the copper and brass pipes and valves that carried the steam were still present. The visibility on the bottom was more than 8m, so we decided it was unnecessary to deploy a guideline. However, my buddy did hang a strobe light on the down line to make it easier to find for the ascent. Now began our real exploration of the wreck, and we swam in the direction of the stern.

TRIP ALONG THE SWIMMING POOL

The wreck had decayed and fallen apart through the years; thus, we had to pay attention to the sharp edges of the hull plates that were scattered about on the sea floor. One of the plates was still standing upright, and square portholes were still clearly visible in the wreck. Several metres beyond, we saw the same portholes sticking out of the sand. These probably served to bring light to the saloon or the dining area. Several years ago I saw similar bronze portholes on the wreck of the SS *Tubantia* in the North Sea, indicating that these were used a lot in that period on passenger ships. These days it would be unthinkable, and too expensive, to equip a ship with such materials.

When we continued our exploration, we discovered pieces of a floor covered with bright green tiles. Apparently, these were remnants of a swimming pool, which made it abundantly clear that money was no object when they were building this ship. Next to the swimming pool we found part of the mosaic tiles of the showers. Further along towards the stern I recognised one of the capstans, probably driven by

Mosaic bathroom floor.

Capstan.

steam. (These served to pull in the lines and hawsers during the mooring of the ship.)

Directly aft of the capstans we found the rudder mechanism with the axle to which the rudder was connected. We had reached the end of the wreck and it was about time to make our way back. We swam past two large engines, where I took my last pictures before starting the ascent. The start of the ascent after a deep dive is an important moment and before we started I made sure I had replaced the cover on the dome port of my camera so as not to damage it. During the decompression it is necessary to focus only on this task and not make any mistakes. Everything went according to plan; we resurfaced after more than an hour and had a happy reunion with the dive ship that was awaiting our return. The excellent visibility and the variety in the different parts of the wreck certainly made this a memorable dive.

Rudder.

Portholes.

THE SS *LAURENTIC*

THE RECORD SALVAGE OF 43 TONS OF GOLD

The salvage of the SS *Laurentic*'s gold had
been one of the most difficult jobs the salvage
team had ever performed: after seven years, it
had managed to salvage 43 tons.

SS *Laurentic*

Type: Passenger ship
Built: Harland & Wolff, 1908
Owner: White Star Line
Propulsion: Three propellers and steam engine
Tonnage: 18,724 tons
Length: 172m, beam 20.5m
Speed: 16 knots
Passengers: 1,600

The luxury passenger ship SS *Laurentic* was completed in April 1909 at the historic Harland & Wolff shipyard in Belfast. The ship was built for the White Star Line prior to the yard building its Olympic class ships, *Britannic*, *Olympic* and *Titanic*. She was built with three screws (propellers) rather than the conventional two, and a steam turbine driven from the exhaust of the two conventional engines as an experiment to improve speed and efficiency, later implemented on the Olympic class ships.

The ship would serve the route from Liverpool to Canada, and was the biggest ship on that line. However, when the First World War broke out it was commissioned by the Canadian Expeditionary Force and modified to become an armed cruiser.

A RICH CARGO

On 25th January 1917, forty-three tons of gold were loaded aboard the *Laurentic*, which was to serve as payment from the British government to the United States

Previos page: Six-inch deck gun. (Photo: Darragh Norton)

and Canada for ammunition and wartime supplies. While in Liverpool, the ship was loaded with the gold, making Captain Reginald Norton a little anxious about the journey ahead. He therefore made sure the precious cargo was stowed properly in the second-class baggage compartment. After a final briefing with his officers, the mooring lines were released, and the SS *Laurentic* started its journey across the Atlantic for Halifax, Canada.

Underwater photographer Darragh Norton.

Gold bar.

While around the north-east coast of Ireland, the captain received his first setback when the ship's doctor reported an outbreak of yellow fever. Four sick people needed to be taken off the ship as soon as possible, and the nearest available port to drop them off was the Irish naval base at Buncrana, close to a small fishing port and roughly 18 miles from Lough Swilly. As the ship closed on

A timetable of regular sailings.

Lough Swilly it struck two mines that had been laid by German U-boat *U-80* and sank to the bottom of the ocean. Of the 475 officers and ratings on board, 354 young men lost their lives that fateful night.

SALVAGE FEVER

Shortly after the sinking, the first plans were made to salvage the gold. However, the wreck was in an area where the ocean waves ruled, and the depth also played a big part. The wreck rested at a depth of 43m, meaning divers had to pay attention not to be crippled by the dreaded caisson disease (decompression sickness/the bends). The gold ingots each weighed 10kg, and were stored in a secure room deep inside the wreck. Hence, the ship serving as working platform was placed precisely above the site. Once in position, twelve admiralty divers started the heavy job of opening the wreck. This did not go as smoothly as planned as the divers' path was blocked many times by obstacles and junk, and the depth meant only short bottom times were possible. When after a few weeks the divers finally reached the gold, they successfully brought back some of the ingots to the surface.

The boiler. (Photo: Darragh Norton)

The ship's bow. (Photo: Darragh Norton)

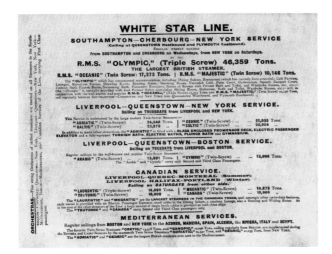

A book advertising the Canadian service.

The Lounge.

The drawing room.

By now it was November and the winter storms had set in, one after another. The divers were forced to stay on shore until the following year and a new diving season, but unfortunately they then found the wreck had been largely ripped apart by the heavy winter storms.

The gold that was once so close was again out of reach. It took weeks of backbreaking work before the first blocks were found. The need to carry out heavy labour under water left some helmet divers suffering from the bends in their joints and they required treatment. As a result, dive times were shortened, bringing on more delays. In total the salvage lasted seven years from 1917 to 1924, and 3,186 bars of gold were recovered out of the 3,211 in the wreck. When the rewards became less than the cost to keep the salvors at work the operation was stopped. However, it earned its place in history as the largest amount of gold ever recovered in one salvage operation.

LAST ATTEMPT

The salvage company Risdon Beazley had become famous after the Second World War as a salvor of precious cargos from sunken ships and it became interested

A postcard of the liner.

Recherche des Trésors engloutis pendant la guerre
On évalue à 50 milliards la valeur des navires coulés par les mines et les sous-marins allemands

Divers working on a shipwreck.

in the wreck. After a short review the company decided to salvage the three valuable bronze propellers, as it would have been too expensive for them to try a last attempt at recovering the remaining gold. These propellers were removed with the help of explosives. Then in 1965 local divers bought the wreck from the Admiralty and often arranged diving excursions to the wreck. In 1986–87 a last attempt was made to recover the remaining gold, but this ended in failure.

LAURENTIC'S GOLD.
THREE YEARS' WORK
NEARLY £4,000,000 SECURED
LONDON, September 15

Twenty fathoms down, among gravel, sea slime, and weird marine forms of animal and vegetable life, naval divers, during the past three years, have been extracting nearly £4,000,000 in gold ingots and silver specie from the twisted steel wreckage representing the once-proud 15,000-ton White Star vessel, Laurentic, which a German submarine torpedoed off Lough Swilly in January, 1917. When the salving of the vast treasures on board—variously estimated at £8,000,000 to £10,000,000 —is complete, the formal story of the diving operations will surpass in romantic interest the wildest imagination of fiction.

A newspaper report of the Navy operation.

LAURENTIC'S GOLD.
£2,250,000 WORTH RECOVERED
(Elec. Tel. Copyright—United Press Assn.)
(Australian and N.Z. Cable Association).
LONDON, August 14.
Of £7,000,000 worth of gold ingots lost when the steamer Laurentic was sunk, £2,250,000 worth has so far been recovered.

LAURENTIC'S GOLD.

ONE THIRD RECOVERED.

(Received 1 p.m.)
LONDON, May 2.
The Admiralty salvage steamer Racer, engaged in recovering gold from the wrecked Laurentic off the mouth of Lough Swilly, is making large hauls of the £250,000 worth of gold still at the bottom when the season's work began. Almost one third has been salvaged by divers.—A. and N.Z.

142

DIVING THE *LAURENTIC*

Nowadays the wreck is a popular location for technical divers such as Darragh Norton, who shot the pictures for this story in 2006. The wreck has been largely ripped apart due to the explosives used by the salvage companies. At various locations you can still see the salvage equipment on the wreck. The boilers, and the triple expansion engine with its experimental turbine are clearly recognisable, and the forecastle is also reasonably intact. One of the large guns was salvaged and has received a new prominent spot onshore as a monument.

The SS *Laurentic* will always be remembered for the most spectacular and successful salvage of gold in history.

DIVE SCAPA FLOW

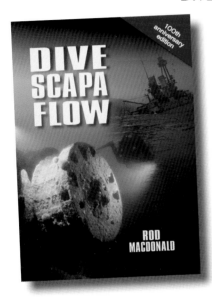

...the ultimate dive guide to the fabulous Scapa Flow... **Scuba Zone**

No...wreck-diver...should be without this book... ...its vivid meshing of history with diving narrative, at which he is a master... ...this new version...benefits in particular from the latest generation of sonar scans, which reveal exactly how the wrecks appear today. **Divernet**

...a superb book. ...guarantees that the definitive guide to diving Scapa Flow will remain exactly that for many years to come. **Undiscovered Scotland**

GREAT BRITISH SHIPWRECKS

...this is a revealing and absorbing read. Written by hugely experienced diver Rod Macdonald, the book highlights almost 40 of the best known wrecks around the UK – including the remains of the German High Seas Fleet scuttled at Scapa Flow. ... Fascinating stuff – with an appeal for divers and non-divers alike.
Scotland Outdoors

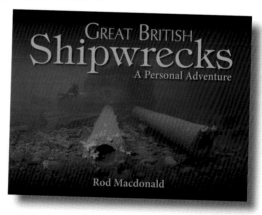

...what makes this more than just another wreck book is the painstaking and thorough research Rod provides. He goes to extraordinary lengths to uncover details about the ships from their builders, owners, crew and the circumstances of their sinking. ... This book is both good to look at and a good read, I thoroughly enjoyed it. **Scottish Diver**

...one more fascinating, easy-going read that comes with sketches and well-shot pictures. ...covers battleships, submarines, ocean liners, along with different equipment, machinery and cargo... Good choice! **Tech Diving Mag**

DIVE TRUK LAGOON

...readers of his previous books will know they are in for a treat. ...a well-crafted history of the area and the American attack. This is an interesting read, with strong attention to detail and use of imagery, ideal for history buffs and divers alike... **Nautilus Telegraph**

A new wreck bible. ...I was hooked. ...this book has it all... ...will appeal to all wreck-divers and is a must if you're thinking of going to Truk. I found it hard to put down as it continued to bring back memories of my own trip. **Diver**

... is arguably the definitive guide. ...essential reading for anyone planning a trip to this remote part of the world. ... It's a rich and hugely detailed work... For anybody planning to travel halfway round the world and see what lies beneath Truk lagoon for themselves, it's pretty much a must-read. **British Diver**

DIVE PALAU

Indispensable guide to wreck diving in this remote Pacific atoll. ...this is as near a definitive wreck diving guide as you'll ever read. ...the level of technical research in this book is breathtaking. ...a phenomenal record. ...brings an almost forgotten piece of war history firmly to life... If you have an expedition planned, read Rod's book before you go. **British Diver**

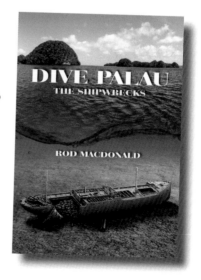

...a rather magnificent coverage of an action taken on 30 March 1944 in WWII on the island of Palau. ... has managed in such books to admirably blend a combination of historical research, capable writing, and excellent illustrations. Highly recommended. **Australian Naval Institute**

Rod Macdonald's books are always eagerly awaited, and it is the level of detail that wreck-dive enthusiasts relish. ...I enjoyed this easy-to-read book from cover to cover, but it would work equally well to dip into for reference. **Diver**

WRECKS AND REEFS OF SOUTH-EAST SCOTLAND

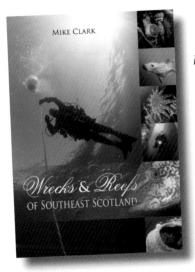

The author has dived all the 100 sites and wrecks, and as a professional underwater photographer has provided truly atmospheric images of these wrecks and reefs. ... Clearly, this book is an absolute 'must' for divers visiting the area. **The Nautical Magazine**

...stunning photographs of wrecks ... a fascinating book which reveals a seabed in rich colour. **Edinburgh Evening News**

...covers a hundred dives and is full of historic details, including newly-found important shipwrecks with photographs and maps and GPS co-ordinates. **Tanked Up**

SHIPWRECKS OF THE FORTH AND TAY

...is a triumph of research and dedication ... will prove to be an invaluable asset to all scuba divers and others who seek to learn more about these vessels and their history. ... For those with a passion for the shipwrecks within the geographical area covered by this work, I doubt a better book will ever be published and I congratulate the author on his attention to detail and painstaking research. **Sport Diver Magazine**

The author has compiled an amazing collection of photographs, some are sinking, some aground, of the ships listed. Typically meticulously, ... has incorporated a detailed index of the exact position of all the wrecks mentioned. **Ships and Shipping**

...a valuable book contributing to the maritime history of the area. Highly recommended. **Sea Breezes**

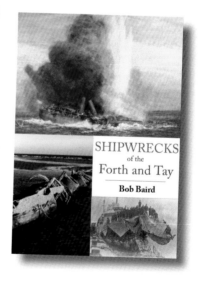

THE FARNES AND HOLY ISLAND

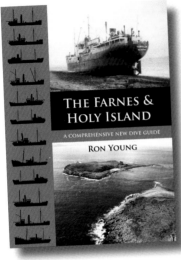

...a weighty and detailed guide ... is a welcome update and comprehensive stand-alone reference. ... The are 178 sites to check out in total, which could take years – a lifetime – to explore. Ron Young has done them all and packaged them up lovingly in a practical, entertaining and thorough fashion. ...buy this book. **British Diver**

...a very comprehensive and thorough guide ... also includes plenty of information about the history and wildlife of the area. ...Ron Young ... has a huge knowledge of all the dive sites. ... All of the wrecks have excellent descriptions... ...this is is an excellent guide book and so much more than just a dive guide. **Tanked Up**

Not only is this a diver's guide but a book of general interest with short histories about the twenty-eight Farne Islands... **RNSA Journal**

THE ULTIMATE SHIPWRECK GUIDE

It is an extended, unique and comprehensive guide to 285 shipwrecks off the North-East coast of England. ... It is bigger and better and definitely more interesting. An excellent book superbly written and researched... ...an absolute bargain, and congratulations to the author for a superb book. Recommended.
The Nautical Magazine

...I regard this work as a triumph of meticulous research and would suggest it is probably the 'only' reference material any wreck diver frequenting the north east of England will ever need and is, therefore, thoroughly recommended.
Sport Diver, Ned Middleton

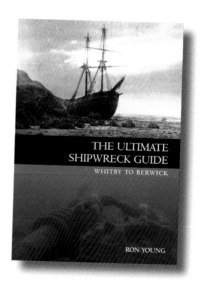

An excellent well-composed book ... A wealth of information is included... Meticulously researched, this fascinating volume is recommended to divers, researchers and historians. ... Highly recommended. **Sea Breezes**